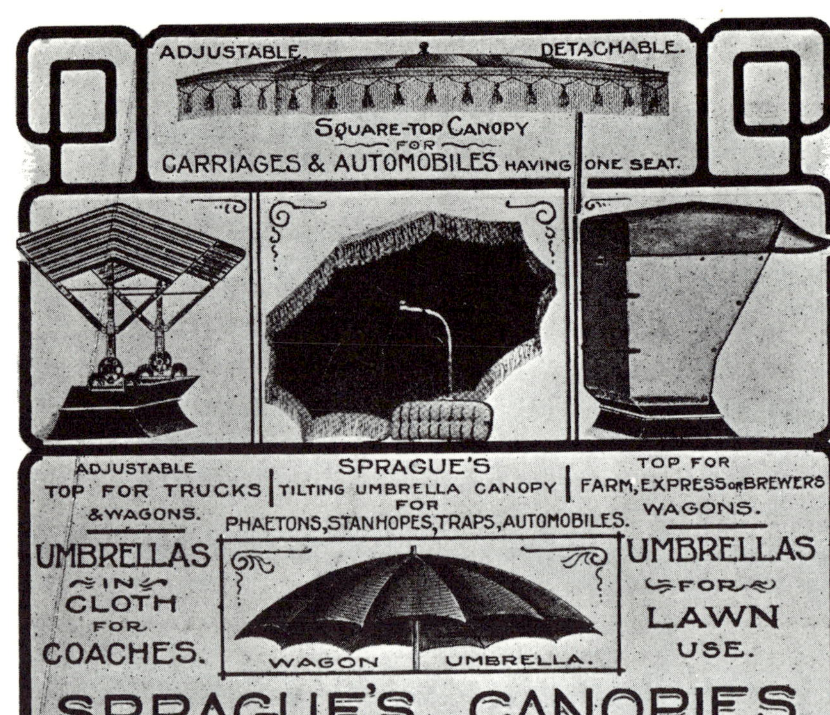

ADJUSTABLE.   DETACHABLE.
SQUARE-TOP CANOPY
FOR
CARRIAGES & AUTOMOBILES HAVING ONE SEAT.

ADJUSTABLE
TOP FOR TRUCKS
& WAGONS.

SPRAGUE'S
TILTING UMBRELLA CANOPY
FOR
PHAETONS, STANHOPES, TRAPS, AUTOMOBILES.

TOP FOR
FARM, EXPRESS OR BREWERS
WAGONS.

UMBRELLAS
IN
CLOTH
FOR
COACHES.

WAGON   UMBRELLA.

UMBRELLAS
FOR
LAWN
USE.

SPRAGUE'S CANOPIES
ARE THE BEST MADE
AND ARE USED ON THE
MOST STYLISH CARRIAGES.
YOUR   SURREY,   MADE UP-TO-DATE BY USING
STANHOPE,
RUNABOUT, ETC.,   OUR CANOPIES.
THE SPRAGUE UMBRELLA CO.
WRITE FOR   CATALOG.   NORWALK, OHIO.
PRICES.

ADJUSTABLE.   DETACHABLE.
SQUARE-TOP CANOPY
FOR
CARRIAGES & AUTOMOBILES HAVING TWO SEATS.

Antique Auto Body
TOP WORK
for the Restorer

by

Herbert J. Butler

Post Motor Books
1970
Arcadia CA 91006

©

Copyright
1970
Dan R. Post

Library of Congress Catalog Card
76-18437

ISBN: 911160-04-3

The Vintage Craft Series

Other manuals in the **Vintage Craft Series** provide authentic ground for rediscovery of other early automobile body building trades. Each volume, written and illustrated in graphic detail by recognized contemporary authorities of that golden era before the Wars, revives one of the key motor body hand crafts in three-dimensional clarity.

VALUABLE REFERENCE FOR EVERY OLD CAR ENTHUSIAST—AND AS HELPFUL AS BLUEPRINTS FOR THE SERIOUS RESTORER!

Preface

Like the wood and leather trades during primitive days of the motor car, top work began as a direct continuation of practices refined with the horse-drawn conveyance.

The first top for a self-propelled vehicle was improvised from an umbrella, undoubtedly handheld. Earliest models did not go in for such frills. The umbrella led to outside manufacture of a more rugged parasol top, supported by a single post curving forward from behind the seat.

An Automobile with Sprague Top attached.   Made in large sizes for two seats.

Alas, severe motion presented new problems. Experience from the carriage realm was drawn upon once again. The extension or cape top was reintroduced, and became early recognized as a more satisfactory solution. Still, buggy top design carryovers occasionally disintegrated in the super-gaited breeze of 40 *mph*. Automobile requirements brought about a fast re-engineering of the buggy extension top, from bow construction to covering. The improved type found universal acceptance among horseless carriages.

In those early years, tops, as well as windshields, headlamps, and even fenders, were categorized as accessories. During that era tops were not built by the auto makers, but by accessory manufacturers — quite often firms

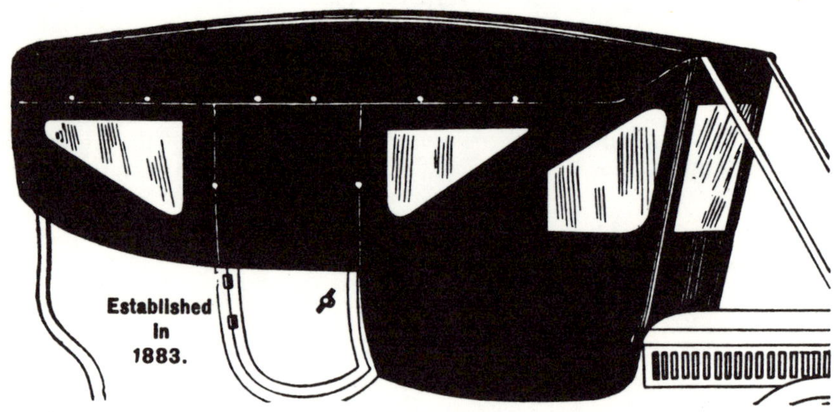

Automobile Tops, Wind Shields, Storm Fronts, Cushions, Backs and Carriage Trimmings of all kinds. Write for catalogue and prices.

BUOB & SCHEU, Court and Spring Sts., Cincinnati, Ohio,

that had cut their teeth on the older carriage trade. Various competitive makes and styles became authentically associated with practically every early car model of the day. Several optional contemporary types of tops often proved popular on a single model. Any of these may be regarded as proper for that particular restoration today.

This book faithfully reproduces top data originally appearing between 1904 and 1926, from such rare American trade publications as *The Hub, The Carriage Monthly, The Vehicle Monthly,* together with an unexpurgated reprinting of pertinent British material: an overview chapter from "Motor Body Work" (1924) by the grand authority Herbert J. Butler, and selected sections from "Motor Body Building" (1914) by the early masters C. W. Terry and Arthur Hall. Some English terminology and spelling should prove a minor hurdle.

Cape or extension tops in a variety of applications — including related styles in carriage form — are described, largely in chronological turn. Successor "One-Man" styles follow in representative variety. From these layouts the precise design, proportion and explicit measurements for a particular top reconstruction today may be determined by the individual restorer.

Selections for this volume were made from the W. E. Miller *Library of Vehicles* and the Dr. Alfred S. Lewerenz Collection.

Dan R. Post, Publisher

Contents

Preface 5

Overview

The Extension Top or Cape Hood / MBW 1924 9

Wood and Metal Bows, Bending Wood, Laying out the Top, Aligning the Bows, Slatted and Tubular Fittings, One-Man Top, Overhang, Determining Number of Bows, Modern Top Mechanisms, Roadster Fittings, Top Fitting Material, Front Fastening, Webbing and Back Straps, Props, Fastening the Folded Top, Separators, Coverings, Making the Top, Back Curtain, Back Fasteners and Turn Buttons, Side Curtains, Front Curtain and Wind Screen, Hinged Door Curtain, Back Seat Curtain, Side Curtains Folding with Top, Concealed Top, Top Boot, Ventilation, Electric Lighting

Background

Development of the Cape Top from Carriage Days / TCM 1904   24

The Extension Top Era

Dimensions from Body Measurements / TCM 1906 34

Early Development, Construction / TCM 1905 37

Bows, Sockets, Joints / TCM 1906 40

Victoria, Enclosed Quarter / TCM 1906 43

Elimination of Front Straps, Production Design / TCM 1906 . . 44

Variant Solution, Non-folding Removable Hard Top / TCM 1906   47

The Apron or Storm Front, Construction / TCM 1906 48

Oiling Old Straps / TCM 1907 51

Victoria Construction, Four Bows, Open Quarter / TCM 1906 . 53

Victoria Construction, Five Bows, Open Quarter / TCM 1906 . 55

Touring Car, Typical Fitting / TH 1907 57

High Wheeler Construction, Three Seat Omnibus / TCM 1912 . 60

Touring Car, Four Bows, Materials to Order / AASC 1909 . . 64

Roadster, Three Bows, Materials to Order / AASC 1909 . . . 65

Commercial Car Construction,
Three Bows, Lightweight / TCM 1913 66

Cabriolet Construction / MBB 1914 69

Convertible Construction, Detachable / MBB 1914 73

Touring Car Construction / MBB 1914 79

Enclosed Cabriolet Construction / MBB 1914 86

Windshields, Wind Screens, Construction / MBB 1914 . . . 87

The One-Man Top Era

Variations, Five Production Styles / TCM 1914 92

Development, Refinements, Construction / TVM 1921 107

Designing, Construction Review / TVM 1920 110

CAPE HOODS

The cape hood consists of a number of bows, bent so as to form an arch over the body, hinged to the body side and usually to one another so that they extend the full length of the body and fold down compactly at the rear. The top and back are covered with waterproof twill and the sides are enclosed with curtains of similar material of various patterns.

The hood must be rigid, yet light in weight, so that it may be easily manipulated, a feature which will be largely decided by the design of the fittings used and the length and width of the body. Adequate protection from the weather can only be ensured by the addition of side curtains which have not only to perform this function, but must be made so that they can be quickly placed in position and detached, allow plenty of light to enter the body, and be arranged so that the sections above the doors open with them, as shown in Fig. 28.

Wood and Metal Bows.

The bows or sticks are usually made of ash or other timber which is suitable for bending by steam. Wood is not unduly heavy and it allows easy fixing of the twill and fittings. Metal tubing of brass or japanned D section steel tubing is also used, but special means, such as a wood filling or straps and staples, are necessary for attaching the hood covering. The metal bow, however, is neat in appearance, it will keep its shape without the addition of stiffening plates, and is particularly suitable when a loose top cover is used, or the hood is of great width.

Bending Timber.

The timber selected from which the bows or sticks are made must be young and straight grained and only partly seasoned, because the steaming process has the effect of completing the seasoning process. The stuff is planed up with a good allowance made for finishing off. As the length of a stick, if straightened out, measures approximately 9' 6", allowing 4' 6" in width and 2' 6" for the sides, the stick, as prepared by the benders, will be at least a foot longer than this. The steam chest to take timber of this size is about 12 feet in length. It is steamed for 30 minutes to an hour, the actual time depending on the cross section and the quickness of the bend at the corners. Experience is necessary to ensure that the sticks are not over steamed and any small defects present in the timber, which may have been overlooked, will be magnified and manifest themselves in the subsequent bending process. When the timber is removed from the steam chest it is bent round a former built up of blocks of wood corresponding to the nine or ten inch radius of the sticks. It is firmly clamped in position and allowed to dry. An iron band is placed along the outside of the timber with the end turned up so as to prevent, as much as possible, the natural tendency of the wood to stretch on the outside and compress on the inside. The stick is first clamped in the centre and then the two ends are bent round their respective formers simultaneously. The cramps are not allowed to touch the wet timber, but shaped blocks, having the required radius on the inside, are inserted between. The drying timber must be firmly held along its entire length, and, although separate corner blocks can be used for a stick with a straight middle, the former or mould will be its full inside length if the stick has a rise of an inch or so in the centre, a design which will assist in throwing off the water when the hood is covered.

Bending may be done by hand and heavy work by means of chains and a winch, but much of the repetition work to-day is carried out by means of special wood bending machines which are designed to distribute the pressure where required. The comparatively high price of bent timber is owing to the fact that it must be selected, and due allowance has to be made for a percentage of wasters. Bows, other than of stock size, should be ordered well in advance, because timber benders are usually busy, the trade being in comparatively few hands. The strainers, which are delivered with the bows to keep them in shape, should never be removed until the timber is actually required for dressing-up.

Setting Out the Hood.

The setting out of the sticks is arranged to give the proper amount of headroom and also to maintain a good outline to the hood. The stick upright by the doorway is mounted so that the underside of it is about 3′ 0″ off the top of the cushion or 3′ 6″ off the top of the seatboard in front. The back slanting stick is set out so that the roof line has a fall of 1½″ to 2″ from the stick just dealt with, and it also projects about the same distance from a square line drawn at the back of the body. The rest of the roof line forward then consists of a horizontal portion to the next stick bearing, after which it slopes down gently to the next one. The chief precaution necessary is to leave sufficient headroom for the front seat passengers, and to preserve a well-balanced outline. From the stick bearing, approximately above the front of the driving seat, the peak then slopes sharply downwards to meet the square line of the extension stick on top of the windscreen, the total drop of the roof line being from ten to twelve inches. The hood of the open touring body usually fits on top of the wind screen, in which case the height of the screen is determined by it.

Dressing up the Sticks.

The sticks will be dressed up to finish about 1¼″ x ⅞″. The actual sectional shape will depend on their position and vary according to the way the fittings are attached. The back stick, for example, requires the hind corner to be well rounded over where the twill turns at right angles, and the front edge of the extension stick is finished off in a similar manner for the attachment of the front edge of the roof cover. An intermediate stick, if it is set at an angle, has the twill bearing suitably flattened. All the other corners are slightly rounded so that there are no sharp edges exposed to tear or chafe the material.

Slatted and Tubular Fittings.

The slats or fingers of the cape hood fitting measure about $\frac{3}{4}''\times\frac{3}{16}''$ half round. They are designed to screw on the outside of the stick for which a flat bearing is provided and the end of the stick is rounded over in both directions below the bottom screw hole. The inside width of the stick must correspond to the overall dimension of the body where the hood folds, with not less than an inch clearance each side. The tubular pattern of fitting, which has the stick shouldered down and inserted into it for a depth of five or six inches, is a popular type in America, but is seldom used here. It demands more substance in the main portion of the stick, but the neat appearance of this style of fitting is utilised to the best advantage when it is combined to form a tubular steel bow.

The One-Man Hood.

The one-man hood fitting is designed in various ways. Its leading features consist of an upright slat to carry a stick well clear of the doorway and one centred to it to carry the back corner, as shown in Fig. 16. The rest of the mechanism may be broadly described as a combination of the cantilever and lazy-tongs principles, the former to support the hood for the greater part of its length and the latter to provide a device which shall automatically extend and contract it. The length of the arms, and the various centres, must be so arranged that they work sweetly in conjunction, and, when the hood is folded down, control the moving sticks so that they lie down flat and parallel to one another and with about the same amount of overhang.

Overhang.

The overhang must be restricted because it spoils the look of the body, and the hood is rendered more difficult to support rigidity. Overhang of the hood in a two seater interferes with the comfort of the passengers on the dickey seat. In a four seater it prevents luggage or a spare wheel being stowed closely to the back panel, unless the hood is raised. Although overhang is objectionable, the main turning centre must be located far enough back so that the sticks turning on it, whose length are decided by the amount of headroom afforded and modified by the shape of the roof line, shall fall clear of the back rail of the body.

The Number of Sticks.

Compactness is an ideal always to be sought, but it must not be achieved by the use of too few a number of sticks as the twill will be insufficiently supported. This will cause it to wear in holes more readily and the water will collect in pools, while at the same time, the shape of the hood will suffer. If the distance between the two main rear sticks at the roof line exceeds thirty inches an intermediate one should be interposed. This may be connected directly to the main fitting so as not to increase the number of centres used. It will frequently happen, however, that a full length stick placed midway between the two above mentioned will not be long enough to reach the back of the body. It is therefore shortened and hinged to the stick above the doorway so that it folds forward on to it, or it may be hinged in a similar manner to the back stick.

Modern Hood Mechanisms.

From the front of the stick above the doorway the horizontal or base member of the cantilever portion extends forwards to carry the extension stick which is fastened to the top of the screen. This is hinged approximately about the centre, so that, when the front is lifted, the whole folds in half downwards against the stick over the doorway, as shown in Figs. 23 and 24. Usually, this centre will also be connected by a diagonal stay running from it to the stick over the doorway, which helps to support the peak of the hood. The centre may also be provided with a stop joint so that it is further supported and can only be moved by lifting the front. The majority of one-man hoods are provided with a short stick which holds up the twill midway between the screen and the doorway stick. This, if hinged to the main horizontal member of the fitting either side of its centre, can be arranged to move automatically in the proper path when opening and shutting the hood. If only a rear centre is used, this short stick may be operated by a stop on a cantilever stay which crosses it. This stick depends on the drag of the twill to pull it into position.

The horizontal portion of the fitting may have only one centre each side on the doorway stick instead of two. In this case it does not form a cantilever and does not support itself, so that, until the front of the hood is fastened on the screen, the twill has to hold it together. The only advantage of this arrangement is that the number of parts is reduced. A good fitting can be designed, however, with only one centre on the doorway stick by providing a second and lower one on the short stick behind it which, in this instance, is hinged to the back stick. With a fitting of this pattern each centre is interrelated, thus every part moves simultaneously and there is a minimum of strain on the webbing and twill.

For a long hood, four points of support, without counting that of the screen, allow a good shape to be given to the hood, for the roof line between any two sticks, since it is formed by a flexible material, must be a line more or less hollow, the degree of which depends on how tightly the hood is fitted and fastened. If the scuttle is of good depth, or the body shorter, three bows are sufficient.

Another method of disposing the sticks is to provide two short inclined sticks instead of one, to support the peak, the longer extension so formed permitting an upright stick to be mounted well clear of the doorway. As

12

Fig. 16.
The Kopalapso Triple Extension Hood Fittings extended.

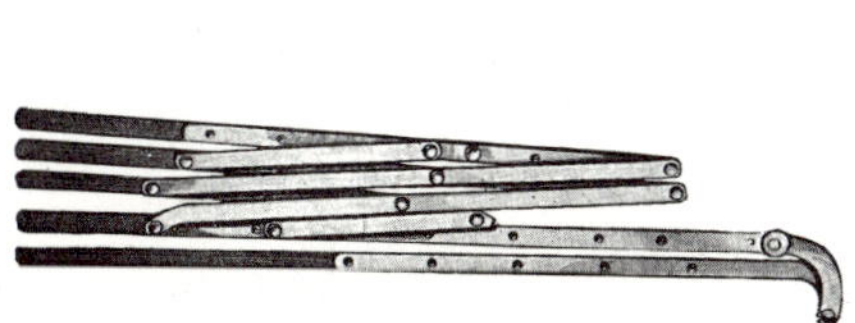

Fig. 17.
The Triple Extension Hood Fittings closed.
The feature of these fittings is the perpendicular
màin stick facilitating the fixing of the side
curtains.

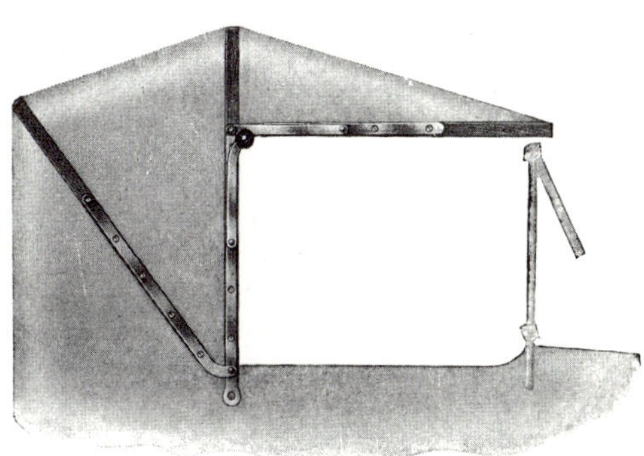

Fig. 18.
The Kopalapso Square Entrance Two-Seater Hood
Fittings extended.

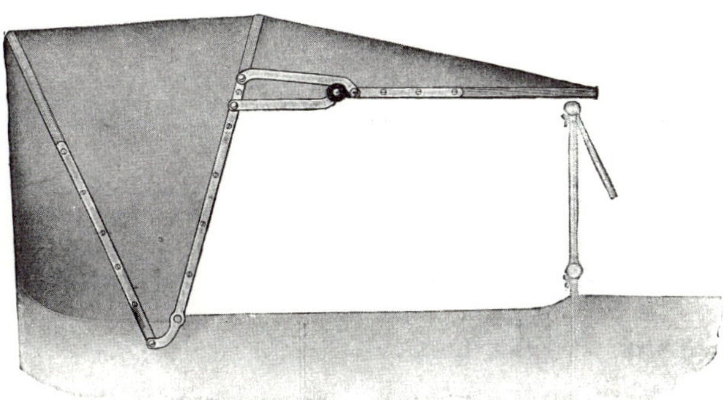

Fig. 19.
The Kopalapso Two-Seater Hood, using three sticks only, for small cars.

Fig. 20.
The Fittings shown in Fig. 18 folded.

Fig. 21.
The Fittings shown in Fig. 19 folded.

Kopalapso Hood Fittings by Messrs. Donne & Willans, Ltd.

there is no direct support for the hood between the screen and this stick, the peak should not be of undue length, because apart from the strain so set up, the hood has to withstand a certain amount of side sway.

The ease of operating any type of hood may be facilitated by anchoring a coiled spring to the main turning centre, or it can be raised by means of a concealed cable and winch, the cable being attached to a bell-crank lever forming an extension of the fitting.

Two Seater Fittings.

The fittings for a two seater car may consist of a pair of slats hinged to a common centre with an extension fitting to give the necessary amount of contraction when the hood is folded. Another slat may be added to carry the twill on the quarter and give a better line to the hood, but this is inconsistent if more than twice the distance separates the top of the door stick from the screen. The back stick is set out to give more drop to the rear part of the hood than with a four seater, six inches being an average. If the front stick is kept closely to the door and upright, it allows an entrance of reasonable comfort with plenty of side protection.

The simplest type of extension fitting consists of a link motion which, os being reversed, shortens the stick an amount equal to the length between it centres. A slide provided on the inside or front of the upright stick may perform a similar function, or the extension fitting may be jointed in the centre with a stop action. Two seater head fittings are illustrated in Figs. 18-21.

Hood Fitting Material.

The hood fittings should be made of good quality mild steel so that they keep their shape. Most of the items have a section of $\frac{1}{8}''\times\frac{3}{16}''$ and are afterwards electro or close plated in brass or nickel or any other finish desired. The fittings are riveted together and care is necessary in assembling them to ensure that each side is drilled to a template and the rivets are of equal compression so that true alignment is maintained.

The Front Fastening.

With the old-fashioned extension hood it was a common practice to hold the front of the hood forward by means of straps or wire cables fastened to staples on the front wings which were bolted through to the flap of the stay underneath. This was seldom a rigid means of fixing, also there was the drawback that a draughty space was left between the top of the screen and the hood. It may be necessary, however, on a two seater car which is only fitted with a single screen swinging from a bottom joint, but as the hood is small, it may be retained by a neat strap only carried to the dash lamp bracket having a hook end and a buckle for adjustment. The top of the single screen should swing closely to the hood and a valance piece of twill fastened above so as to well overlap the top of the glass.

14

The attachment of the extension stick to the top of the windscreen stanchion not only eliminates this space, but a rigid and definite outline is provided for the attachment of the side curtains. It has been an important factor in the development of the all-weather hood.

A popular type of fastening used is the ordinary thimble catch which has a nick in it engaging with a spring-loaded pawl in the other part. This fitting may also consist of a ring or socket-plate screwed to the stick which drops over the stanchions and is then held securely by a bolt and butterfly nut. It will be an advantage if the screw allows of a small longitudinal adjustment so as to pull the hood up tightly and correct any slight distortion present.

The Webbing and Back Straps.

The sticks are kept the proper distance apart by two rows of webbing nailed to them and running the full length of the hood. Folded strips of the hood covering may also be used. If the hood is of extra width, as in a char-à-banc, the number of pieces of webbing is increased to three and additional strands added running diagonally. The back stick is fastened to the body by a pair of straps the upper end being nailed to the top of the stick and the lower end passing through a staple, or better still, a specially made loop bracket. For a heavy hood a pair of V or Y-shaped straps may be chosen and either pattern may have a buckle so that the hood may be adjusted from this end.

The Props.

The hood fitting is centred on a pair of props between a shoulder and the cap-nut provided. The neck of this prop or bracket is cranked out the necessary distance from the side of the body to give the proper clearance for the falling stick. The neck is about $\frac{3}{4}''$ round and the screwed portion $\frac{3}{8}''$ and may be in the solid with the body plate or standard, or the latter is provided with a socket so that the prop may be afterwards bolted on, a method which facilitates the entire removal of the hood. The body plate is of about $1\frac{1}{2}'' \times \frac{3}{8}''$ mild steel with a 6″ cross flap screwed to the elbow and another on the seatframe or other convenient part of the framing.

The back prop or hood carrier is nearly always separately bolted on to the body iron and is shaped in various ways to provide a good bearing for the folded hood. As the elbow rises towards the rear and the bottom line of the hood is lower than its turning centre, the back prop is usually cranked downwards. The bottom is looped upwards or flattened out to a cup shape and often provided with a leather or rubber pad to reduce vibration.

Fastening the Folded Hood.

The prop will also have a staple or loop to take one end of the holding-down straps. An excellent fastening consists of some style of hinged bar-clip the pressure of which can be adjusted by means of a butterfly nut of ample size. A metal fastener is neater and quicker to fix than a strap. A tightly-clamped hood will not rattle ; there is less likelihood of the twill being worn into holes, and it is then more easily covered with its envelope.

Hood Separators.

Pressure on the sticks will not injure the twill if the hood has been well folded and separators are fitted. These are usually made of brass attached to the stick close to the point of clamping and marked off for position when the hood is folded so as to get them directly one above the other. They consist of a male and female portion and are screwed either to the side or inner surface of the stick. A rubber block, hollowed out on both sides and fastened to alternate sticks, makes an inexpensive substitute.

Hood Coverings.

The hood covering consists of various qualities of waterproof twill usually of a brown or khaki shade with a thin layer of rubber inserted in the centre. Imitation leather is also used and real leather is sometimes adopted for the Victoria-shaped heads of two seaters. Waterproof twill is made up in rolls 60″ and 72″ wide, so that there is no difficulty in cutting it out economically.

Making the Hood.

The sticks, before being finally attached to the fittings, are french polished and sometimes covered with twill in the middle portion. They are then mounted on the props and retained in their proper relative position by means of two parallel lengths of webbing stretching from the back rail of the body and fastened temporarily in front, if the wind screen fixing is not available. The webbing is arranged each side within an inch of the rounded corner of the stick and fastened with nails. Two inch webbing is an average size ; and the centre line of it will represent the seam where the centre roof piece is sewn to the two side pieces. The centre piece, having been carefully strained into position, is doubled over before being tacked to the extension stick, and on its back edge to the last stick, where it will join up with the back curtain, ¾″ to 1″ being allowed for turnings at sides and ends. The sides are then fitted from the centre line of the webbing, the bottom line being square with the base of the extension stick and the back edge slanting off along the back stick. A similar allowance is made for turnings, except that double the amount is left on the bottom edges so that it may be turned in twice to form a strong fixing. Care is necessary in fitting the front end of the side pieces because the twill has to be brought round the corner of the extension stick and nicely adjusted to the contours formed between it and the front sloping stick.

After the twill has thus been fitted it is removed and the parts sewn together. The methods of seaming are varied according to the experience of the trimmer, but the centre and sides are usually sewn together first, both pieces lying in the same direction, after which one of them is turned over in its proper position so that the three thicknesses thus formed may be sewn together. Any eyelets required for the attachment of the side curtains are then sewn in.

The Back Curtain.

The back curtain with a ¾″ allowance for turnings at the top, and twice that amount for double turnings at the edges and bottom, is fitted along the

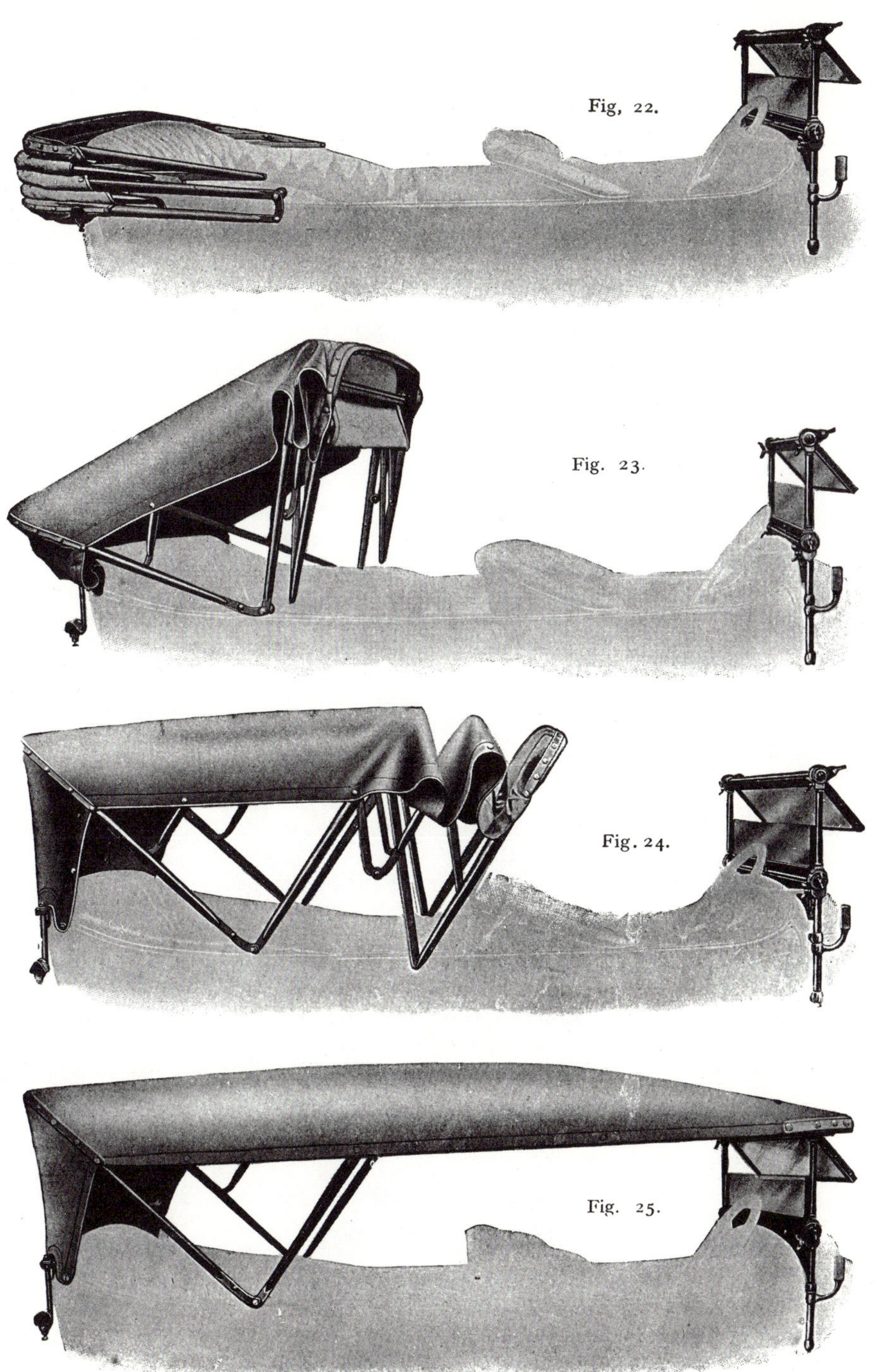

The Kopalapso One Man Hood by Messrs. Donne & Willans, Ltd.   The four views show the hood
from the folded to the fully extended position.

centre of the back stick and drops vertically where it meets the bottom edge of the side pieces and then round the back rail of the body running parallel about three inches below it when finished. This curtain may be varied by fastening it along the full length of the back stick, or a permanent side curtain embraces the whole spread of the sticks by the side of the back seat so that it becomes virtually a Victoria hood. This arrangement reduces the number of curtains which have to be specially placed in position.

The Back Lights.

The design of the back curtain is modified according to the number, size and setting out of the rear lights. It may be fastened on as a single curtain or with a detachable centre panel so as to give extra ventilation when the hood is being used as a sunshade. The back light is inserted to enable the driver to see towards the rear when reversing and to provide a look out for the passengers on this seat. A difference of opinion exists as to whether one or more lights should be fitted. With one central window the driver's view does not tend to be obstructed by the heads of the passengers, who are able to see out without turning right round. On the other hand, two windows give more scope for looking out and break up better the comparatively large area of the curtain. Some firms favour a small single glass light. This looks extremely neat and is more likely to give clear vision after extended use.

Fixing the Celluloid.

Celluloid may be purchased in sheets 24″ x 54″. It is polished on both sides and varies in thickness from one to six hundredths of an inch. The size of the light is set out so as to leave about an equal amount of stuff above and below it. If two windows are being made, the distance between them should not be less than four inches. Having set out the size and position of the opening ⅜″ is allowed inside this to allow for turning in the stuff and the hole cut out. The celluloid is then cut out 1″ larger all round than the finished hole and laid on the back of the curtain. This is fixed by means of a ring of twill placed behind the celluloid finished about an inch wide with both edges turned in. This is made by cutting a hole in a piece of twill ⅜″ smaller all round than the sight size of the light and then cutting out a frame of stuff 1¾″ wide. The light is finished by running two parallel seams right through the curtain and back piece with the celluloid in the centre. The celluloid may be large enough to take both rows of stitches or only the inner one.

Glass Lights.

The fixing of a small bevelled glass light is done by means of a split metal frame fitting together with the twill clamped between the two halves. The outer frame is rebated to take the glass and both are drilled to take metal thread screws put in from the inside which holds all the parts together. A new pattern has a tongue and groove formed in each half of the frame respectively, which thus provides a joint to hold the fabric more securely.

Fasteners and Turn-buttons.

The hood cover is then fastened on with tacks, the copper variety preventing rust. The tacks are hidden with banding and studs covered to match the hood, or with brass bead, a material which is nearly always used for the front extension and the junction of the top and side pieces with the back curtain. The back curtain is fitted with a row of eyelets to engage with the turnbuttons screwed to the back rail. The eyelet to take the turnbutton is in two portions, the outer one being fitted with prongs which turn over and are clinched to a corresponding plate at the back. The turnbuttons have necks of various lengths to accommodate one or more thicknesses of material. A side curtain is attached to the free edge of the hood at the top by various kinds of snap fasteners. These must be strongly made and of ample proportions, if they are to prove satisfactory, and not come undone with every gust of wind.

Side Curtains.

The design and number of side curtains used varies according to the arrangement of the doors, the shape of the permanent portion of the hood, the position of the wind screen and whether they are detachable or otherwise.

Of primary importance is the exclusion of rain, therefore the edge of the top cover comes below and in front of the top of the curtain. Working from the front each curtain is fastened so that the back edge overlaps and lies on top of the next one to it. A special valance-piece is sewn on inside the top cover to take the upper fixing for the curtains. This valance can be brought lower above the doors and reinforced with a stiffer material so that a lip is provided for the hinging curtain to shut against. A door curtain cannot be depended upon to push itself under the top cover in the process of shutting even if it has a metal frame and has to be adjusted by hand, so that the top is made just to clear and abuts against this valance.

The Front Curtain and the Wind Screen.

As the front door usually hinges on the forward pillar and the wind screen stanchion is in line with it, the mounting of this curtain is a simple matter, but care is necessary to make a weather-proof joint. This is done by making a pair of metal clips. These are welded or riveted to the curtain frame or standards and embrace the screen stanchions where they are screwed on with a good lap of twill to cover the joint. A hinge may also be made by fastening turnbuttons to the stanchions with metal thread screws, or instead of fixing these directly to the stanchion, a special plate, hinged closely to the side of the screen, may be provided for attaching them. If the screen is permanently inclined, the top edge should not project beyond the doorway and the front curtain is carried forward to meet it, the bottom edge being suitably shaped to conform to the contours of the scuttle. If the door is hinged on the back pillar, then a small narrow curtain is required between the screen and the door. This is difficult to make up satisfactorily as the door curtain must, when closed, have its front edge behind the smaller curtain so as to keep out the wet.

The Hinged Door Curtain.

The door curtain is made up on a frame of $\frac{1}{4}''$ or $\frac{5}{16}''$ round iron to which cranked feet are welded, engaging with sockets screwed to the back of the door. A rigid frame all round provides a good shutting surface at the top and gives more scope at the bottom for setting out the feet to suit the door framework. This will be an advantage when the curtain is much wider than the door, an arrangement which saves the use of a separate curtain between the front and rear doors and gives easier access to the body. A cheaper way of mounting the curtain is to have a pair of side rods only. These can be attached by sewing on a strip of stuff with a double row of stitches. The rods are then held in the slots formed between the rows of stitches and the curtain can be pulled off them at any time it is not required, and stowed away in a very small space. Should the second doorway open from the front pillar, it is made in one with a fixed portion at the side of the driving seat and forms an excellent hinge. This plan is also suitable for a single central entrance, the curtain then extending to the wind screen with a small flap on the off side for the driver's use.

The Back Seat Curtain.

The detachable curtain fitted at the sides of the back seat passes behind the hood sticks and joins up to the back curtain, see Figs. 26 and 28. This makes a neater job than bringing it outside the sticks which is necessary if the back curtain is fastened to the full length of the back stick.

Regarding the size of the celluloid panel used, the tendency is to make it as large as possible, so that the twill forms a framework only. If the celluloid is divided into a double row of horizontal panels it can be folded along the line of division and gives an uninterrupted view along the top where it is most wanted.

Side Curtains Folding With the Hood.

Instead of detaching the curtains and making them to hinge with the doors, various devices have been invented to stow them away without removal. One method consists of fitting the curtain with narrow vertical lights and threading its top edge on to a wire cable fastened to the inside of the sticks. Each curtain is then bunched up and swung under the top of the hood where it is held by straps on a clip. The Hall curtain is mounted on a wire, but each curtain swings bodily into the roof; the door curtain, however, is hinged in the usual way. Another type designed by Mr. Hillman of Messrs. De Dion Bouton Ltd., consists of a single curtain running the full length of the body and strung on a wire. When it is desired to enter the body, the curtain is simply pulled along to the required position. These curtains have narrow vertical lights, and when folded up, are held in a couple of loops fastened to the back stick.

Another curtain is held at the top with fasteners in the usual way, but it is also connected at one end by an eyelet to a short length of rod running

Fig. 26.
De Dion English H.H.H. Open Touring Body with hood up, and all-weather curtains in position.

Fig. 27.
The above body with hood down, showing curtains being stowed away behind back squab.

Fig. 28.
The Wolseley 15 h.p. Open Touring Body, with hood up, and all-weather curtains in position. Doors open, to show how access is unrestricted.
Photos supplied by Messrs. De Dion Bouton, Ltd., and Messrs. Wolseley Motors, Ltd.

parallel inside the rounded corner of the stick. This arrangement allows the curtain to be unfastened, turned at right angles and run up the curved rod, after which it is rolled up and strapped to the stick.

The Concealed Hood.

When the hood is concealed the body must be curved out specially to enclose it, for if set inwards to maintain a normal exterior, it will decrease the seating accommodation. As the back or longest stick has to lie inside the back panelling, the back curtain is often canted inwards. If of the usual shape, then the hood is arranged to slide forward as a whole, or if it is mounted on a second centre which has the effect of foreshortening it. The hood is concealed behind the usual $1\frac{1}{2}''$ thickness of outer framing with a $\frac{5}{8}''$ board on the inside for the attachment of the trimming and end pieces of similar material. Sufficient clearance must be allowed at the sides for the folded hood with its twill, a larger dimension usually being required at the rear. This horseshoe-shaped box or channel should have a $\frac{5}{8}''$ bottom of hardwood as it not only takes the place of the back props but the box has no internal support and should therefore be as shallow as possible. The lids of the hood-box are shaped to give a handsome effect to the rear of the body.

A simple plan for a small hood is to make a hood valance form the lid. Other methods consist of having two side and one back lid, when the shape is not suitable for hanging as one piece. The rear portion of the box may be dispensed with by arranging the squab to hinge forward to allow the hood to fall down behind it. In all concealed hoods the shape of the folded head should be specially studied. A fitting should be chosen which allows the sticks to fall directly above one another in regular graduations so that the box does not have to be made an inch or two wider at the back merely to accommodate the length of one stick. The concealed hood, as shown in Plate V, gives a neat and appropriate finish to a flush sided or sporting body. It requires care in handling and usually suffers because it is put away in a damp condition. The bottom of the box should be drilled and have communication with the open air through the bottom-side or other part.

The Hood Envelope.

A hood, if not concealed, should be fitted with an envelope or well-fitting bag slipping on from the rear to protect it from the dust which is churned up at the rear. Hood envelopes are shown in Figs. 10 and 11. A hood is very much like an umbrella, for it is apt to be worn out by being folded up too much rather than by actual use. The cover consists of a top and bottom piece and a border connecting them. The shape of these parts is ascertained from the folded head and the twill is cut out with an inch allowed for turnings. The seams are usually piped and the bottom piece is attached to the same turnbuttons as the back curtain. The turnbuttons must be of sufficient strength and length of neck to take both these items. The front edge of the top piece is strapped down to the seat board.

Less dust is created at the back of the car if the top of the envelope is tucked down behind the body and joined up to the bottom piece, so that a free

22

air space is provided between the body and the folded hood. This tends to destroy the usual vacuum which is the chief cause of the dust raised.

Ventilation.

A hood is designed to prevent the entry of the rain, but some form of ventilation is desirable. If the curtains slide, this is arranged on the " leeward " side by drawing one back a little. A panel may also be fitted in one of the curtains to hinge inwards from the bottom and provided with triangular end pieces arranged to fold inwards. These are held open by a couple of light straps and press studs.

Electric Lighting.

The fitting up of the hood with electric light is accomplished by means of a special type of festoon lamp which is mounted in a neat barrel for screwing to the underside of the stick. This barrel has a revolving shutter, the movement of which switches the current on and off and also protects the lamp when the hood is folded. The flex must be armoured and carried by the most direct path to the accumulator. If a lamp is not often required, an ordinary bulb may be used with bayonet fixing. The base is screwed to a piece of stiff leather which is slotted for a pair of turnbuttons. The female portion of the plug, which is permanently connected to the accumulator, is at the side of the back seat and the male portion is fastened to the end of the flex which is conveniently run down an adjoining stick.

Peculiarities of Top Joints, Shapes, Positions and Lengths.

The history of top joints, as we prefer to call it, has never been written, but is very interesting from a carriage maker's point of view to go back for over a hundred years and see the gradual changes occurring from time to time in its shape and position on the top. All carriage tops dating back to the end of the eighteenth century have five bows, and the top joints were all considerably curved. All such tops were made from hides (not split), consequently the leather was thick, stiff and heavy, and the further the bows were apart the more the leather sunk between the bows. As a rule, the five-bow tops were in use till 1840-1850, but four-bow tops were made as early as 1820, used on cabriolet phaetons of the light kind, drawn by one or two horses. This information we have gathered from a colored drawing sent to us by George N. Hooper, of London. In the same collection is a steel engraving of a single crane barouche chariot which was designed, engraved and colored expressly and exclusively for *Le Beau Monde,* or *Literary and Fashionable Magazine,* published in 1810 We find curved top joints similar to a landau leather top. The finish of this side quarter looks as if it were covered with leather, but there is a sword case in the rear, indicating that it is a stationary top, but has a considerably curved top joint, and the strange part is, that this regular landau top joint breaks backward, same as our buggy top joints, and must be, if the top is stationary, a mock top joint only. We

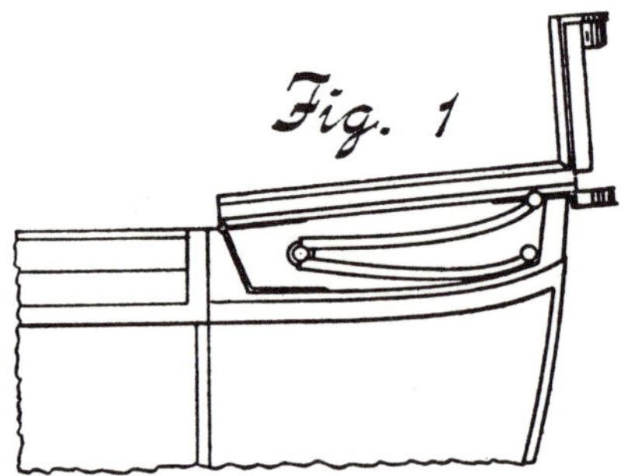

notice that in all top joints, from about 1800-1860, very little change occurred in shape, and for sixty years these extreme curves were in fashion.

We notice that also all caleche tops with four or five bows, from 1800-1835, were higher front than back; but 1830 the change started to lower the front bow and raising the rear one. In 1835 the front bow was only a trifle higher, but in 1860 the difference was 2 inches, and has been made so to this day.

In 1825-1830 we note in the collection of George N. Hooper's drawings that the cabriolets and landaus had small oval side lights similar to those used for back and side curtains thirty years ago in this country. At the same time on some of the landaus the back bow had a drop of 4 inches. The change from the curved top joints toward the straight ones occurred about 1860. On a victoria designed by George N. Hooper, 1860, the top joints have a slight curve only, but in 1864 the straight top joints were made on landaus of the very latest styles. As late as 1876 the straight top joints were still made on landaus on foreign and American work, but the tendency has been for curved top joints for landaus, cabriolets and victorias, but carriage builders have never attempted to go into the extreme curves as made from 1800 to 1830.

For buggies prior to 1865, all top joints were made with most excessive curves. Not satisfied with a half curve, the curve started

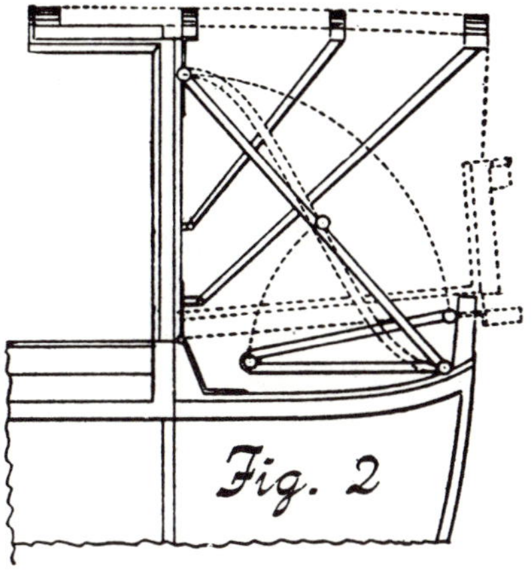

again on props, top and bottom, and a complete scroll was the result on both ends. These extremes were made on light work till 1860, but from that time gradually grew straighter. But in 1866-68 some were slightly curved only, while many were made straighter, till in 1870 all top joints and light and medium carriages were straight, and have continued to be made straight till this day, with the exception of some wholesale manufacturers preferring slightly curved joints.

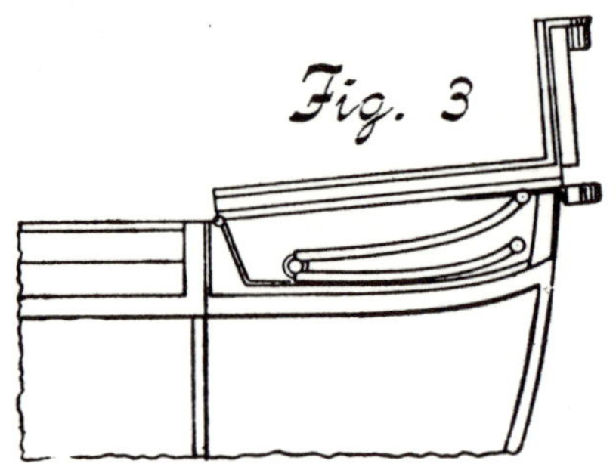

In 1865 the first three-bow top appeared on a cabriolet. This was a novelty, and looked extremely odd at that time, and it took nearly ten years before the four-bow tops were discontinued.

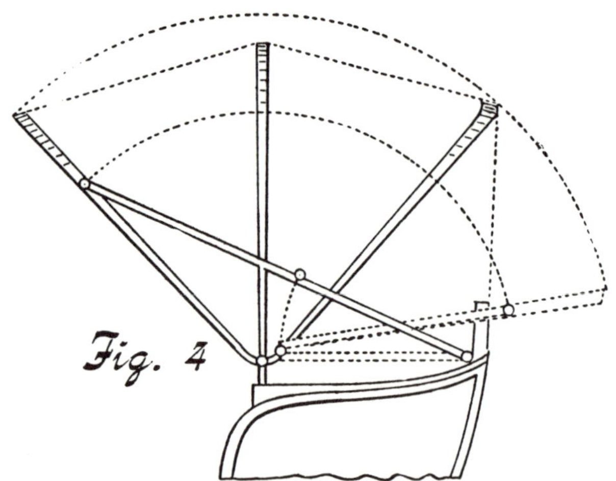

In 1873 the first three-bow buggy top was made in Philadelphia, but was considered a failure from the fact that all trimmers made their tops circular round, and to obtain this result the tops were filled with hair and wadding between the top leather and lining. For this reason the tops did not fall flat at that time. The trimmers attempted to do the same thing on cabriolet tops where the space between the bows was greater, and consequently required a great deal more hair to obtain the shape. The result was that the hair shifted and lumped when the top lay flat, and when up was unsightly.

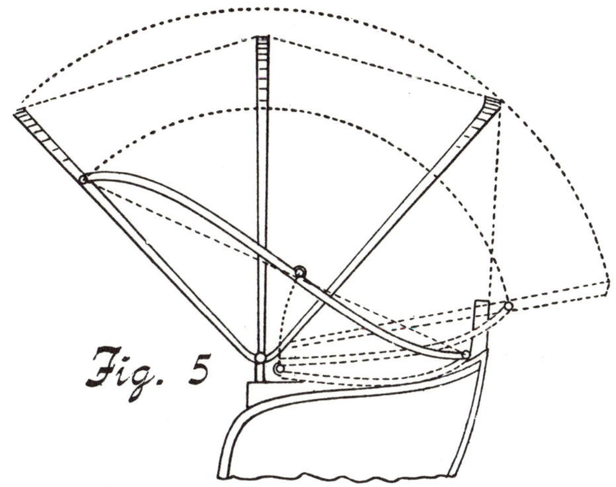

The trimmers at last got out of their old habits of finishing tops. The three bows became popular, and at the Centennial exhibition a great many of the buggies had three bows, and they were all made right, and hardly any change has been made since that time.

POSITION OF TOP JOINTS.

All old top joints, when folded, had the knuckle or knuckles for double joints, and were either between the two props or above. Judging from old drawings made in 1800, the upper knuckle is on a level with the front prop when the top is down, but this is not the case on the Lafayette carriage, which is supposed to have been built about 1815. On this carriage the position of the joints is considered the right position at the present time. But this does not alter the fact that the general tendency was with almost all carriage builders that the knuckle joints should be raised similar to Fig. 1, but a great deal more exaggerated.

By examining well-made drawings, 1860-1865, Fig. 1 illustrates the shape and position. In 1860, the center of knuckle joint was a trifle above the lower prop, as indicated in Fig. 1, but the joints were more curved. This information we have from correct English and French designs. At that time the English coach builders led the nations, and the French followed up to 1862, when they started to improve on the English styles. In 1864 the French dropped the knuckles on landaus somewhat, but at the same time introduced the straight joints, and the position of these joints, as made in 1864, were made the same as made at present, and Fig. 2 illustrates the position of the joint when up and down. Fig. 3 illustrates the

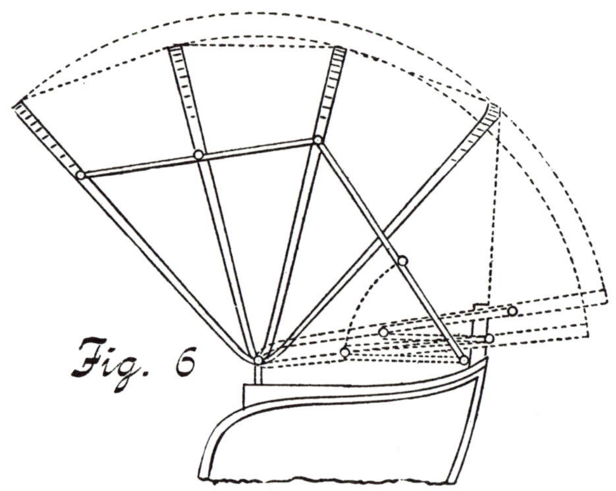

Fig. 6

landau top joints, as made at the present time. Fig. 4 is the three-bow top, as introduced between 1864-1865, including the position of top joint up or down. With Figs. 6 and 7 we illustrate the four-bow cabriolet top with straight and curved joints. With Figs. 8 and 9 we illustrate three-bow buggy tops with straight and single joints, and why not made. If we examine the single straight top joint, with top up, its appearance is not so objectionable, but its defects are such which will show the reason why it is not practicable for light work. One reason is its length for the size. If we would make a top joint the length as illustrated in Fig. 8, and make it the same size

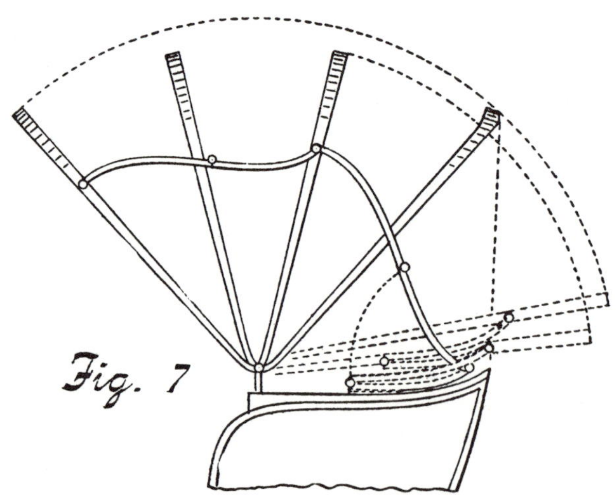

Fig. 7

as usually made on buggies, the strain on the top to pull it over would bend the joint sideways, and would be far from being satisfactory. Note, when the double buggy joints as they have always been made, the strain is divided and the joints are shorter. The long joints tighten the back part of top, and the short joints push the front over, and being horizontal, it does this without the least exertion.

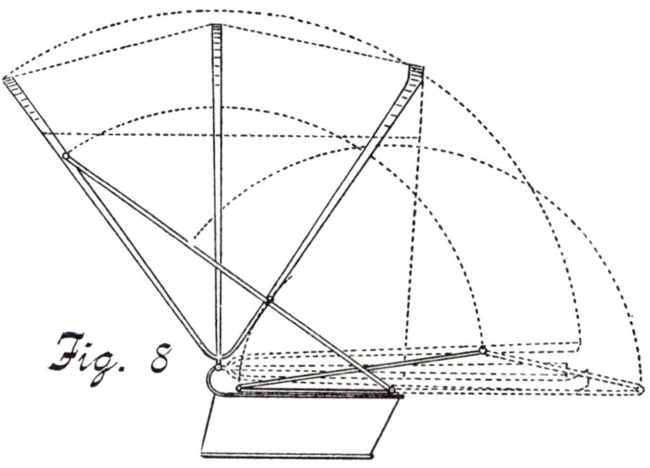

Now, note the effect when the top is down, the joint, when folded back or forward, is so long that the appearance is bad either way.

If we examine the curved joint, its appearance is better when up than the straight joint, but when down it is far worse, and especially so when folded backward. The above explanation in connection with the illustration will be sufficient reason why such joints are not made.

Fig. 10 shows the present style of three-bow buggy tops with straight joints. The bottom prop on seat should be as far back as possible and 1½ to 1¾ inches above the lower edge of side quarter on middle bow. The prop on front bow should be ⅛ inch lower than the prop on middle bow. Now fold the bow, as shown by dotted lines. This should be the position of the finished top, and also the position of the joints. Some assert that the long joint should be perfectly horizontal, but that the knuckle is about ⅛ inch above this horizontal line, and makes a better appearance on the finished job. If made level, it has the appearance as if it dropped, and, besides, it is always liable to drop.

Fig. 11 is exactly the same top as Fig. 10, but it has curved joints.

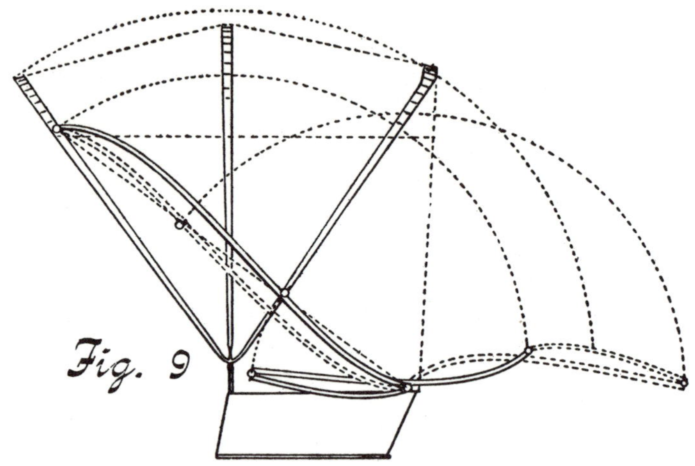

The curved joints look well when the top is up, but not when it is down. There is no difference between straight or curved joints with reference to the length and position of knuckles. The center of knuckle of the straight line will not stay closed when the top is up. This is illustrated in Fig. 9. This method is all right for drawings, as shown on illustrations, from Fig. 1 to 12, but for practical purposes it will not do.

The second method is to obtain the length of joints when the top is up, and position of knuckles when the top is down. The third method is to obtain the length of joints and position of knuckles when the top is standing, and without folding it.

Taking the length of joints and position of knuckles when the top is lowered, we will explain by using Fig. 12. Cut 12 loops the shape as shown on D; the large hole must fit the prop and the small hole the twine or string. Put the loops on as we do the joints. Tie a string to each of the six loops; now fasten the other ends of the strings to the other six loops. These twelve loops, with the tightened string between, represent six joints, three on each side, when the top is up; now fasten B to C on both sides and throw the top, as shown by dotted lines. Fit block between the bows the size to suit the position the finished top will assume when down, which the trimmer knows best from the quality and stiffness of the material to be used for trimming it. Now pull out each string and put knuckle as shown on E, F and G. On each of the strings where the center of the knuckle must be, take a short piece of string and make a knot. Do the same on both sides, and mark each string "right" or "left."

30

Take a board, as shown on Fig. 13. Take all the strings, as
shown, and give to the blacksmith to make the joints by. If he is

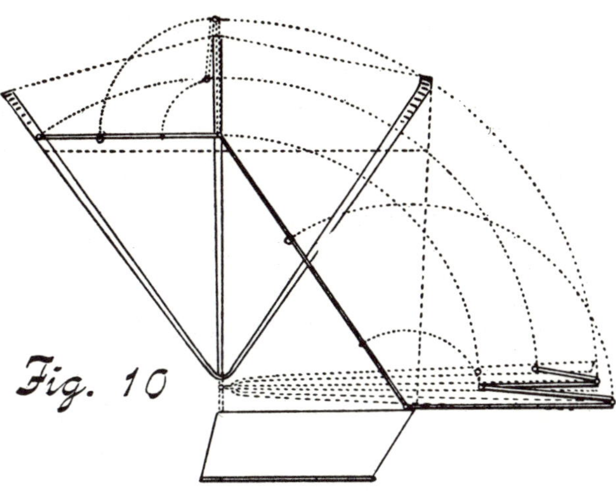

accurate in his work, the joints will fit, and if they are a trifle out
either in length or position of knuckles, a little fitting will rectify
everything.

TAKING THE LENGTH OF JOINTS AND POSITION OF KNUCKLES WITHOUT
DROPPING THE BOWS.

Make two sticks, 3-16 x 1 inch, 3 feet long, bore a hole at each
end of the stick the same size as the prop. The first stick should be
put on prop B, and fitted to H ; get exact center between A, B ; punch
it with the brad awl, put second stick on prop K, lay against joint A
and punch the brad awl through that. Then take length of joist,
same as above; plug hole K about 1 inch long, move it over, as
shown by dotted lines; pull the string, as shown on M. The length
and difference in the length of the two parts is exactly the same as
if the bows were folded. For joint N, we take only the difference
between points B, C, H and O. If these centers would be equal
in length the joint would be directly in the middle. The folded top
shows how the second bow moved back, and consequently affects the
joint. The front end is the shortest and the rear end is the longest.
If we would reverse B and C, or the opposite from what is on the
draft, the front end would be longest and the rear end shortest.

For taking the rear joints, we use the same method. Fit your
stick to lower and upper prop. Plug the upper one, move it down
in the position as shown by dotted lines, and do the same as with
the rest, as explained above. Either of these methods is practicable,

31

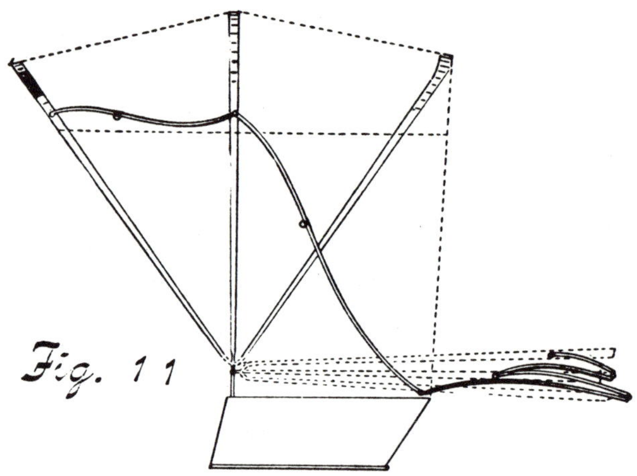

and the only two ways by which the length of the joint and position of the knuckle can be taken. Get a small board, put a tack on upper left corner of the board, hook the loop over the tack; do the same to the left; stretch the string and fasten the tack; also put a tack on the knuckle joint; put the right joint on top and the left on the bottom. Do the same with the middle and back joints; always the right on top and the left joint on bottom, and always front ends to the left.

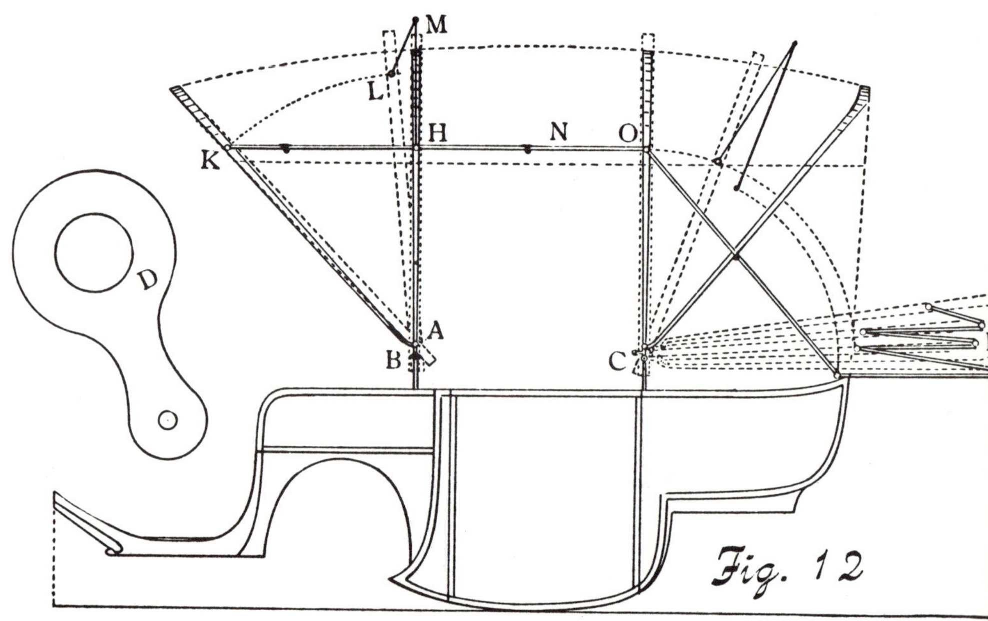

32

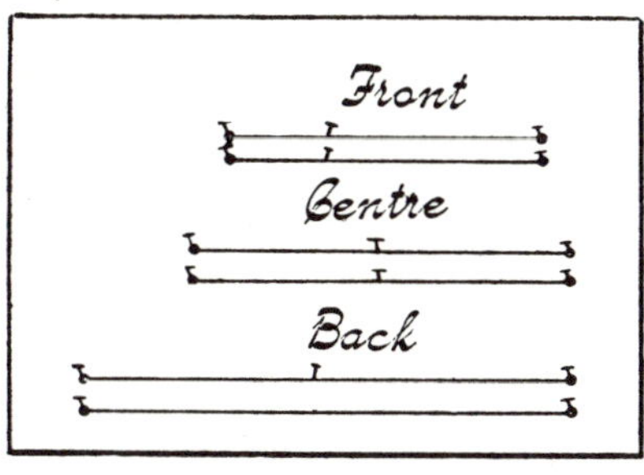

Fig. 13

EXTENSION TOPS AND HOW THEY ARE FOLDED.

Extension tops are made at present with four bows, three folding joints are necessary on each side to support the top. They are all made with straight or curved joints. The front bow moves at A and the second bow moves at B. A moves, but is riveted and moves around the rivet. On B the bow moves, but is fastened with a nut. Suppose the top is desired to be folded. The nuts are loosened on B, moved over to C and bolted together on each side. When the top is down it folds in the position as shown by dotted lines.

The rules for folding the joints are the same as on all tops for light and medium work. While these extension tops are generally built to fold, as shown by dotted lines, they are very seldom folded, and it is considered entirely too much trouble to remove and replace the nuts and front part of top.

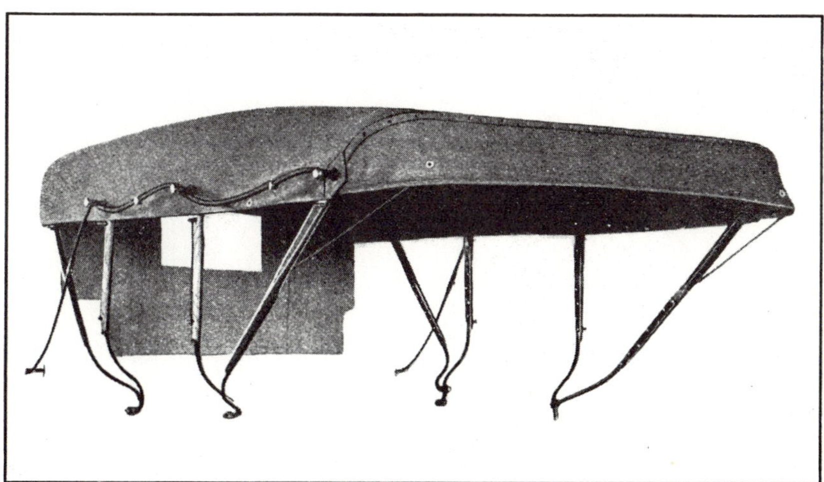

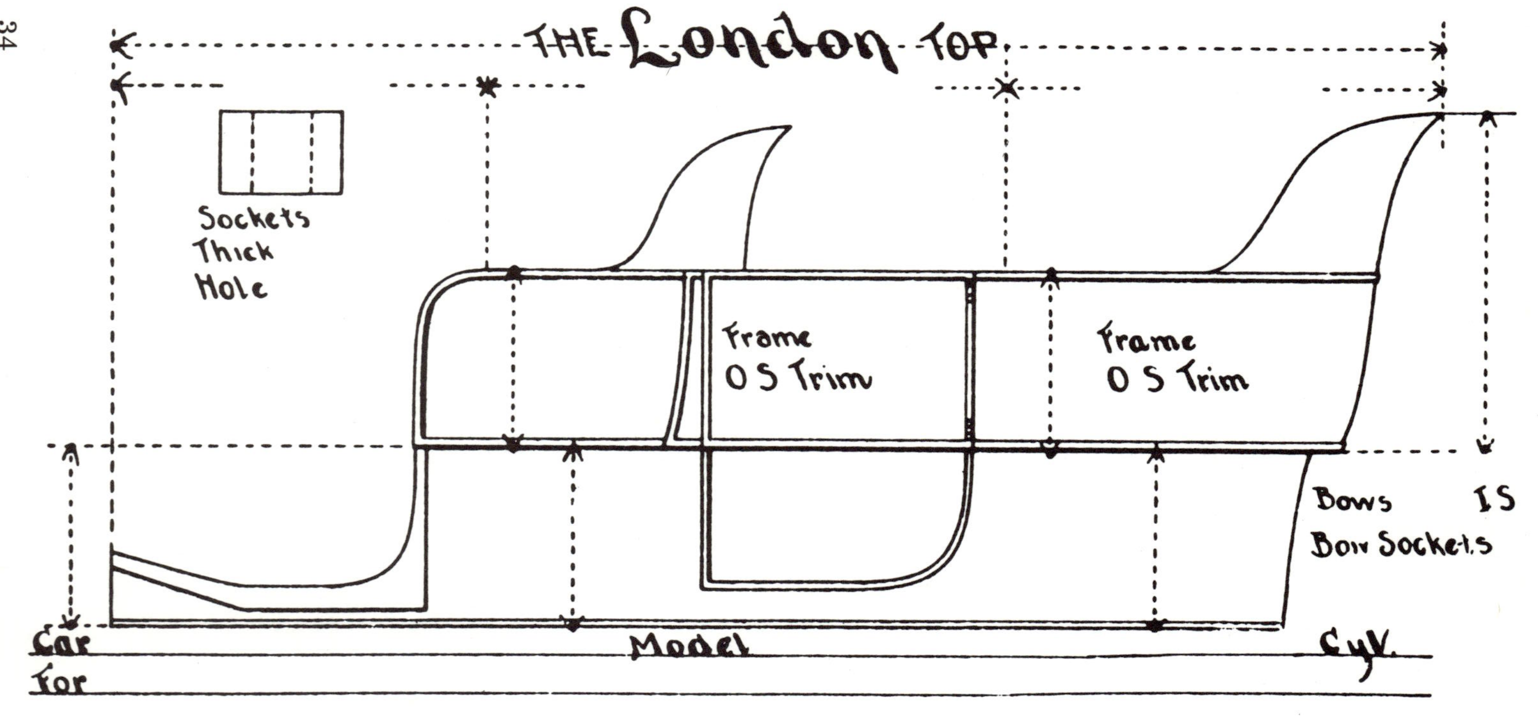

Drawings furnished by the London Auto Supply Company, Chicago, circa 1906, provided the customer with a simple form for indicating pertinent body measurements—a helpful aid for the top builder in determining dimensions for construction to special order.

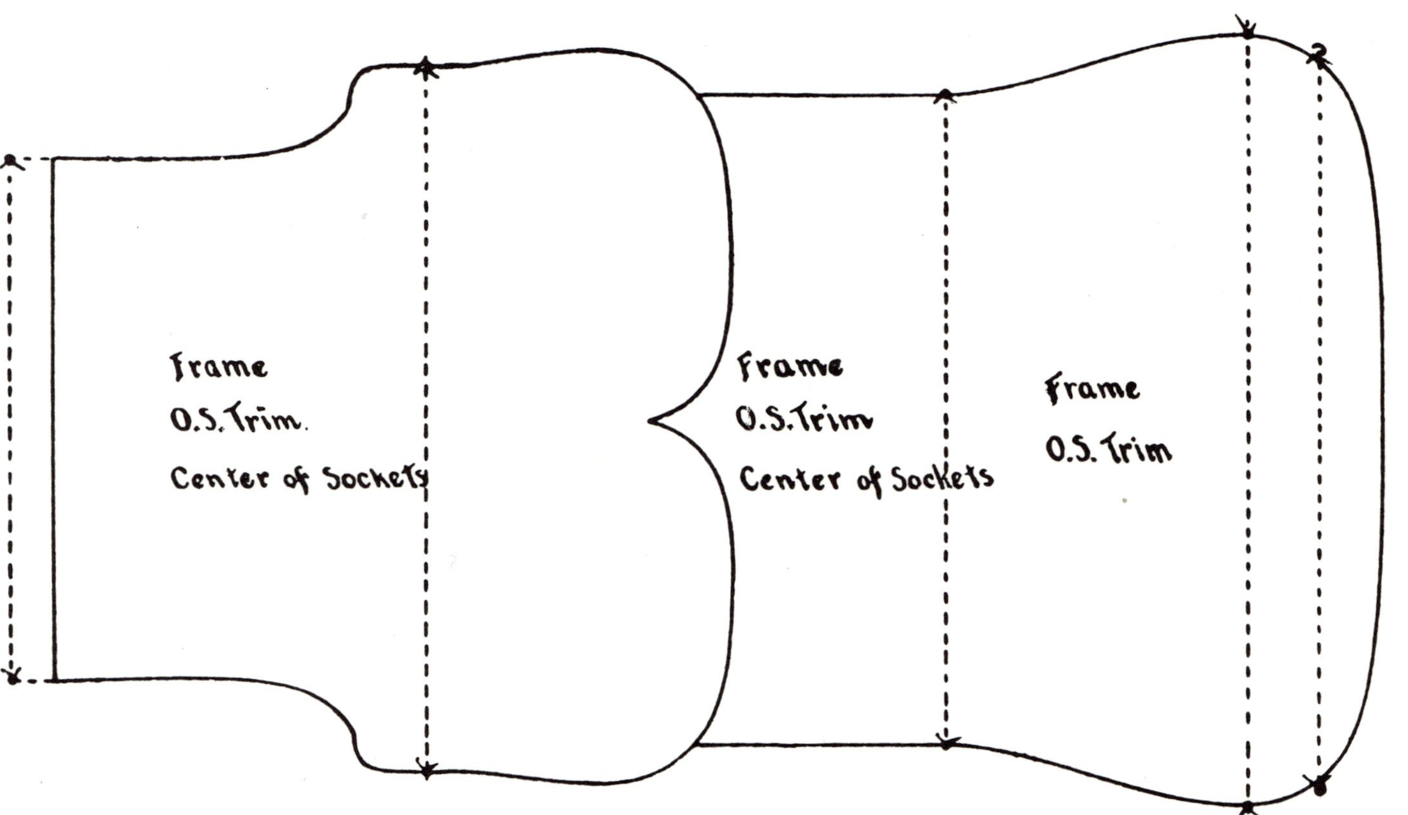

Frame
O.S. Trim.
Center of Sockets
Frame
O.S. Trim
Center of Sockets
Frame
O.S. Trim

TOPS, AUTO

We manufacture Automobile Tops to order. Send measurements as per diagram below.

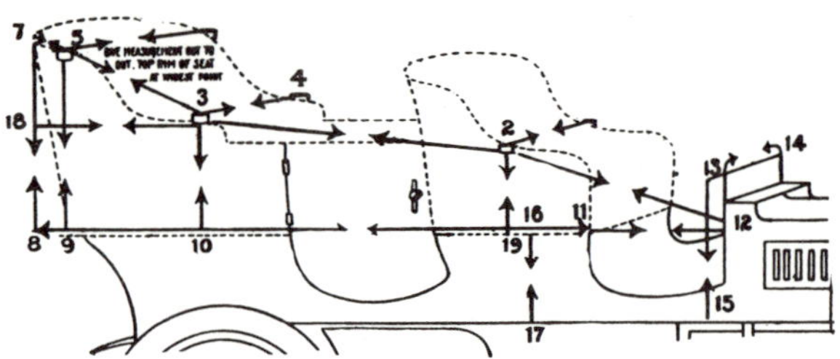

2 to 2—Center to center of body iron......
2 to 3—Center to center of body iron......
3 to 4—Center to center of body iron......
5 to 5—Center to center of body iron......
3 to 5—Center to center of body iron......
5 to 9—Center of seat iron, starting at 5 to bottom of seat at 9................
7 to 8—Extreme top of rear seat, starting at 7 to bottom of seat at 8............
3 to 18—Center of seat iron, starting at 3 to 18 ....
3 to 10—Top of seat iron, starting at 3 to 10
2 to 19—Top of seat iron, starting at 2 to 19
13 to 14—Dash width, 13 to 14..............
2 to 12—Center of iron at 2 to front edge of dash at 12 ....
13 to 15—Top edge of dash at 13 to bottom edge of body at 15.................

16 to 17—Bottom edge of seat at 16 to bottom edge of body at 17 ....
11 to 12—Front end of seat at 16 to bottom edge of body at 17 ....
11 to 12—Front end of seat at 11 to front edge of dash at 12 ....
8 to 11—Extreme end of body at 8 to front end of seat at 11.....................
5 to 7—Center of body iron at 5 to extreme end of body at 7 ....
NOTICE—Measure widest part across rear seat ....
State whether body irons have taper or straight holes, and give size of holes, ⅝ or ¾ ....
Give make of Car and Model ....
Year when built ....

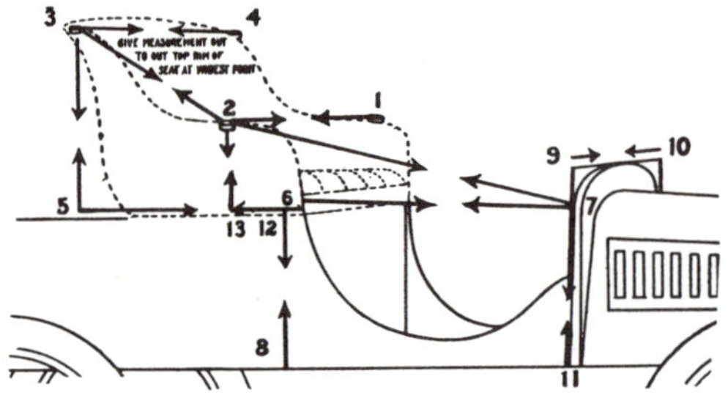

NOTE—Put measurements at end of each line.

1 to 2—Center to center of body iron......
3 to 4—Center to center of body iron......
9 to 10—Width of dash, out to out ....
2 to 13—Top of body iron, from 2 to bottom of seat at 13....................
12 to 8—Bottom of seat, from 12 to bottom of body at 8 ....
5 to 6—Extreme end of body, from 5 to front end of seat at 6..............
3 to 5—Top of iron, from 3 to bottom of seat at 5 ....

2 to 3—Center to center of body iron ......
9 to 11—Top edge of dash, from 9 to bottom of body at 11 ....
2 to 7—Center of body iron, from 2 to front end of dash at 7...................
6 to 7—Front end of seat, from 6 to front end of dash at 7 ....
Notice—Give measure out to out, across rear of seat, at widest point.
State whether body irons have taper or straight holes, and give size of holes, ⅝ or ¾", or if ironed for rail, state......
Give make of Car and Model ....
Year when built ....

Novel Extension Top for Automobiles.

Carriage and automobile builders have been studying to provide a suitable top for automobiles. The extension top was adopted to some extent, but was not suitable for many styles. The cape top was an improvement, and has met with favor and looks well, and

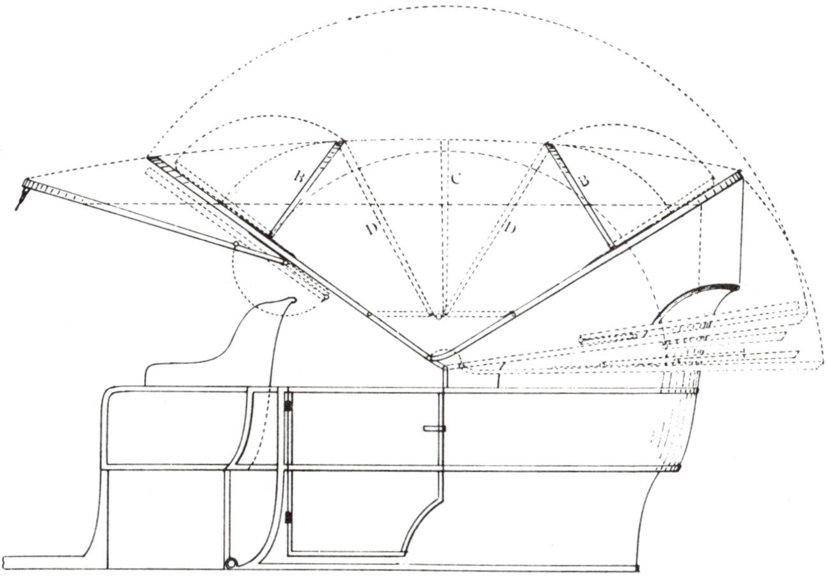

Novel Extension Top for Automobiles.

can be used for either rear or side doors by throwing the top in either direction. A top has been made in France similar to the cape top, but instead of the two middle bows starting from the slat iron they are hinged to the front and rear bows, and the direction is vertical starting from the bows.

The deficiency in these tops is that the two inside bows do not throw over the rear of seat, consequently must rest on top. The seat is high and the bows bulky, and this construction prevents the riders looking sideways. To obviate this, the position of the vertical middle bows has been changed to slant, by which means these short bows extend further toward the upper part of the bows. This construction enables all the bows to drop over the back seat.

The body, on which this top is placed, is of the usual size, but when made shorter, the top is made to suit the length by giving less slant to the bows. If made longer, the inclination of the bows is increased, and a vertical center bow is substituted to avoid the increased space between the bows. The front auxiliary bow can be shortened and lengthened to suit the size of the body. In this illustration A indicates the slat iron support on which the bows move. This support is bent outward sufficiently to allow the bows to drop over the back; or, in other words, the inside width of bows must be one inch wider than the width of seat. This will give ¼ inch play room each side of the seat. We have drawn the bows, when folded, in dotted lines, to indicate the position. Suppose the two inclined bows BB are not desired for a shorter top and one center bow substituted, as shown on C. Again, if bows BB and C are not desired, DD can be used, and if the top is wanted longer, bows C and D can be used by dividing them into equal spaces, and all will then drop over the back seat.

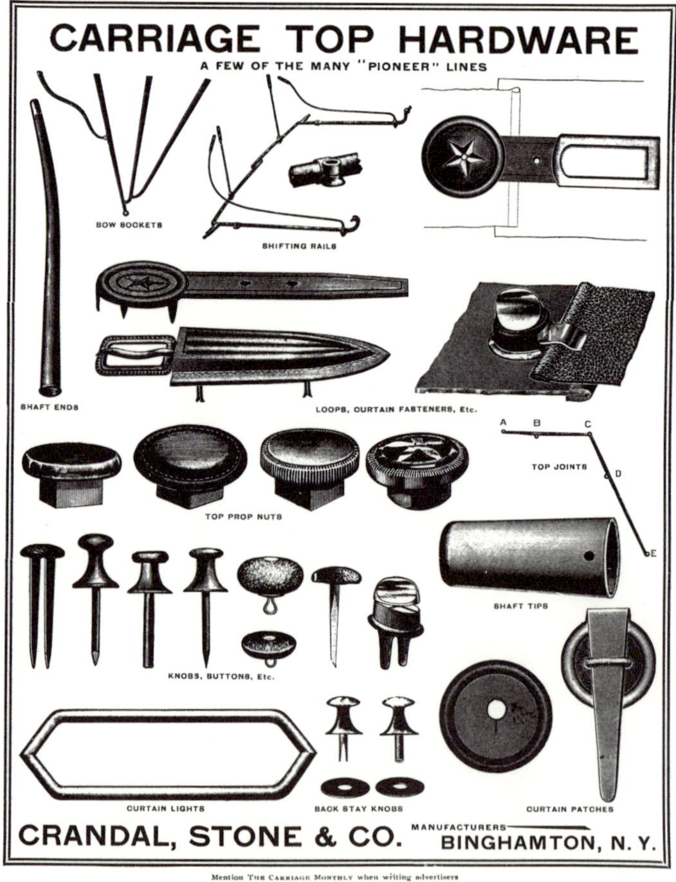

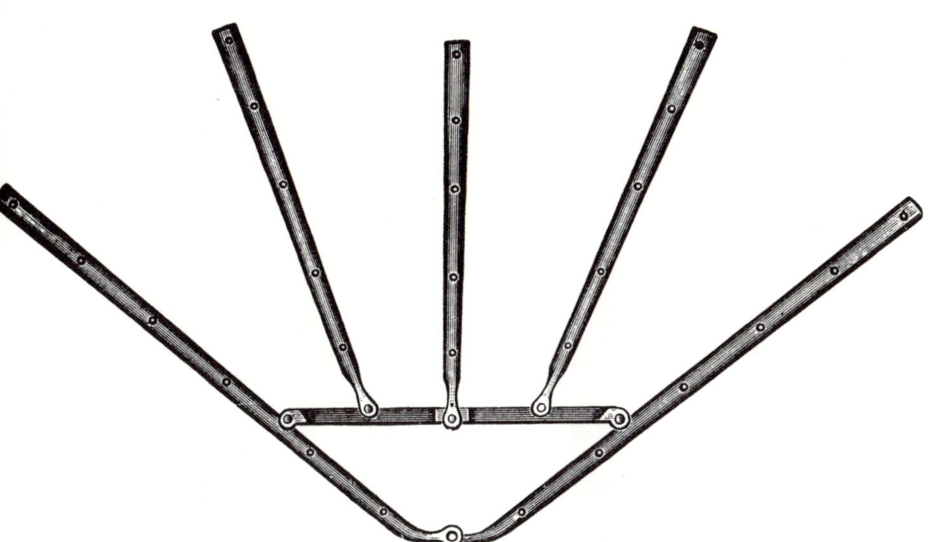

Forged Cape Cart Automobile Slat Irons.

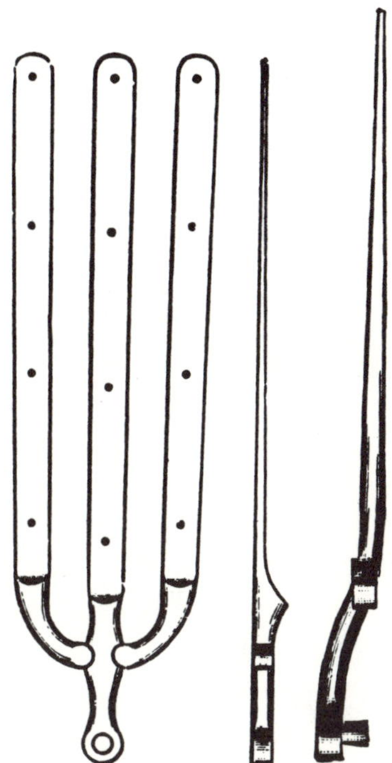

Straight and Curved Three-Bow Slat-Irons.

Automobile Bow Sockets.

Tubular bow sockets have been used on carriages for the last thirty years. They are found to last longer and give more service than the wood and leather covered variety. The strain on the

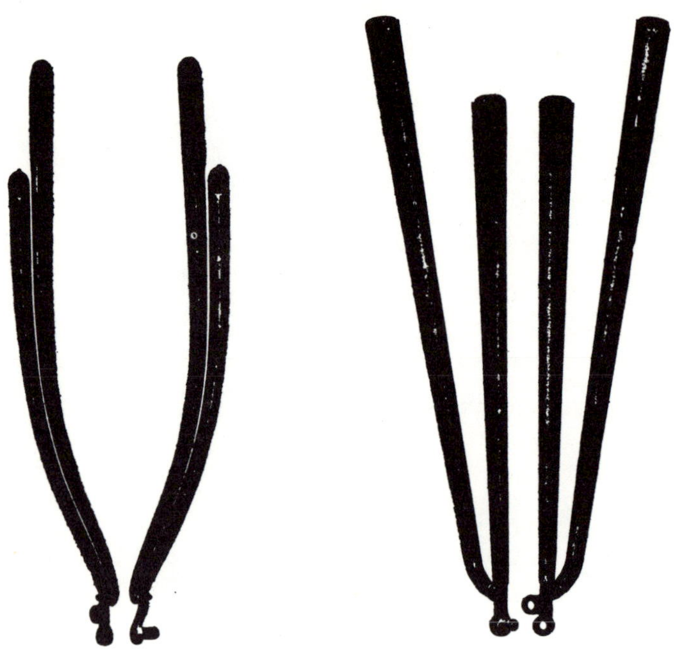

Automobile Bow Sockets as made by the Ashtabula
(Ohio) Carriage Bow Co.

bows is more severe on automobile tops, and, in order to avoid this fact, bow sockets have been introduced, which meet with this requirement. They are made by the Ashtabula (Ohio) Carriage Bow Co.

Well=made Automobile Top Bows.

Automobile top bows differ considerably from carriage bows, because the conditions and the necessary dimensions of such bodies and tops differ entirely from carriage construction. The automobile bodies are higher and longer, consequently the bows are shorter and are further extended in length. One of the most important points to be remembered is that the middle bows are the shorter when compared with the end bows, and too short to be thrown over the back when the top is folded.

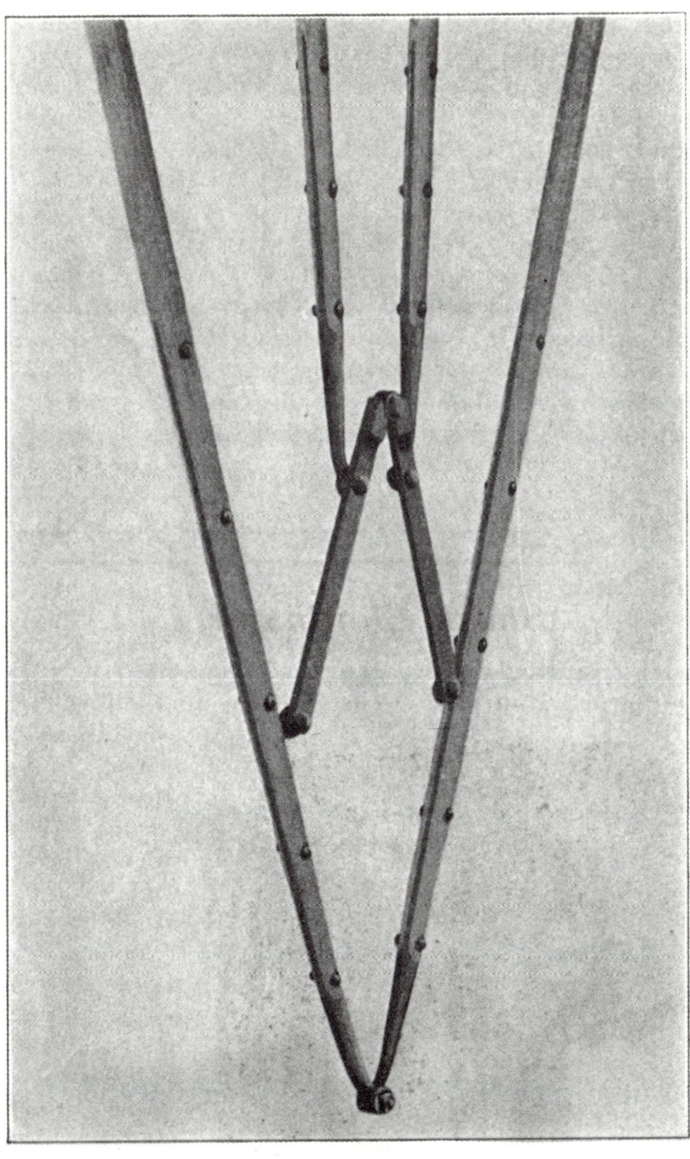

Auto Bows which lengthen the two middle bows to suit the length of body.

The Sprague Auto Tops

Col. Sprague's Exhibit at the Shows
At Madison Square Garden, Space No. 168 Concert Hall.
At 69th Reg. Armory, Space 54 Gallery.
At Chicago Show, Space 140 Gallery.

The
Sprague
Idea

Made
The
Sprague
Way

OUR NEW TOP See the curved irons on the bows. This is the only right way to make the bows; they are straight on the lower ends. The drop forgings will stay in place, and they make a neat, substantial job. See them at the shows. Send for our catalogue.

THE SPRAGUE UMBRELLA CO., Norwalk, Ohio

The Empire Gear and Top Co., of Philadelphia,. Pa., make a top
which overcomes this difficulty. They put a joint between the two
main bows, which is straight when the top is up or unfolded. Fold
the top, the knuckle joints folding upwards, which moves the two
bows with it, making them as long as the end bows. This length is
regulated by the length of the joint between the two main bows. If
the middle bows are too short, move the joint upward, making it
longer, and if they are too long, move the joint downward. The
joint in the illustration is of the right length to throw the top over
the back for a given length of the top.

Automobile Bows.

Automobile bows can be symmetrical and
tasty in appearance, or otherwise. The accompanying cut shows automobile bows of
the former class, as made by S. N. Brown &
Co., Dayton, Ohio. The lower ends are
curved, which eliminates the necessity of a
long arm or goose neck. This bow is finished in the natural wood and is fitted with
brass-plated slat irons; it is durable and
makes a highly presentable appearance,
which is something that counts with the
automobile maker and counts as well with the automobile buyer.

Victoria Automobile Tops.

Victoria tops are built for tonneaus and side-entrance cars by
the C. Z. Kroh Mfg. Co., Toledo, Ohio. These tops are handsome
in design, of a very high quality of workmanship, and are built
to the shifting rail. They can be detached or attached expeditiously.
This company has been building work of this character for the
past thirty years and its adaptation to automobile requirements
comes as an easy matter.

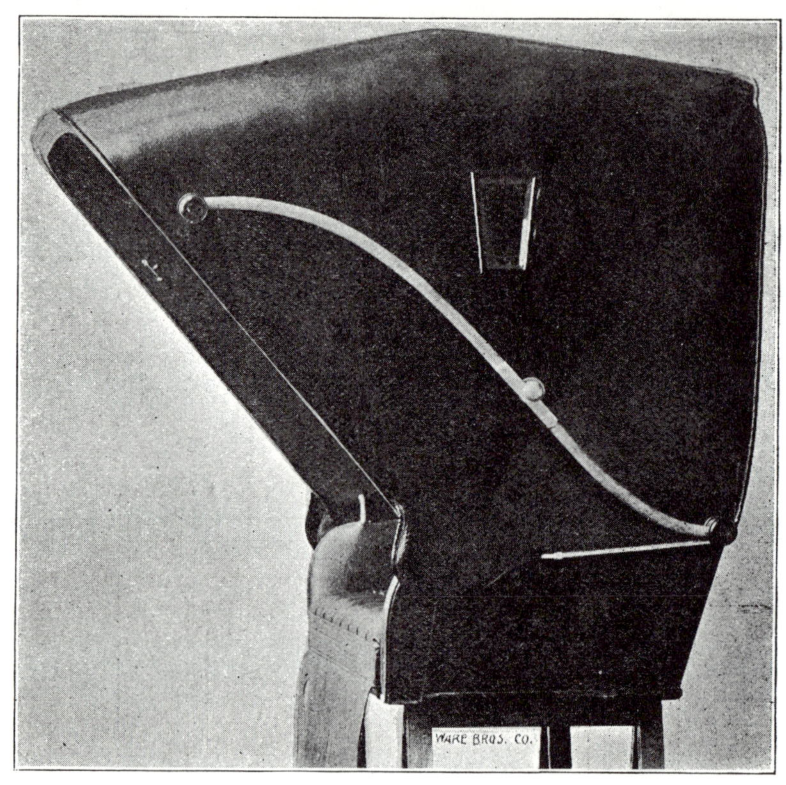

Victoria Automobile Top.

Automobile Extension Tops.

The Michigan Top Co., Detroit, Mich., call the attention of automobile builders to the beautiful outlines of their extension tops. These tops are made absolutely rigid, and do away entirely with front straps. There are arm rests on each side of the vertical bow, which afford the occupants means of steadying themselves while moving rapidly over rough roads. These arm-rests are convenient, and are not seen on many tops.

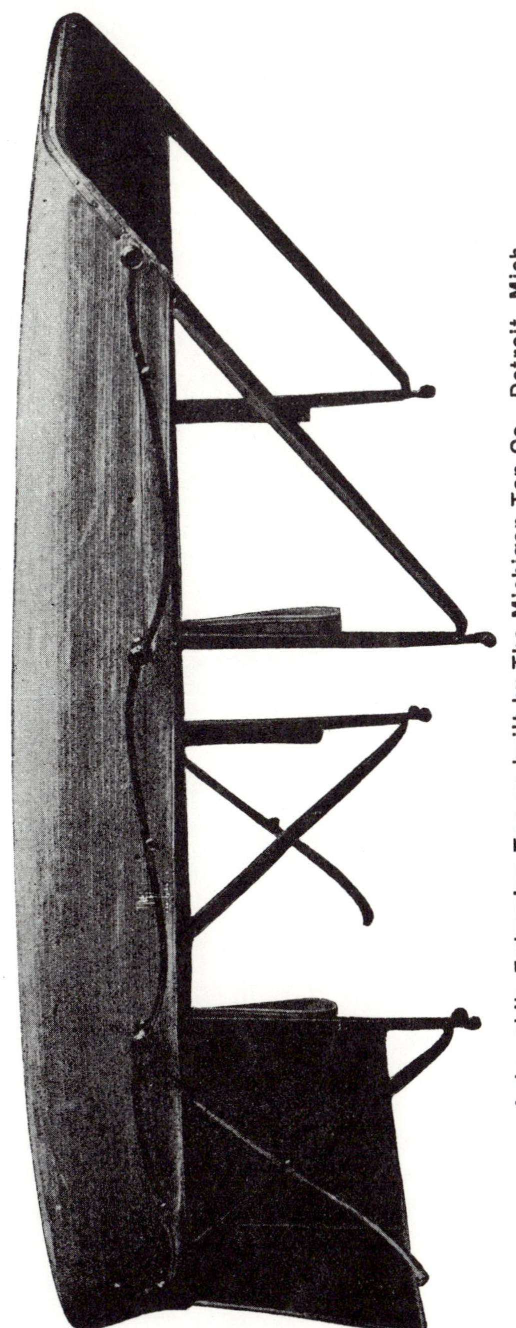

Automobile Extension Top as built by The Michigan Top Co., Detroit, Mich.

Auto Built by Wilson Carriage Works, Phila. H. J. Jacobs, Manager

Folding Tonneau Bodies.

Some very neat specimens of folding tonneau bodies have appeared upon the market, which can be opened to two seats or one, as shown in accompanying cuts. The larger shows two seats

for four passengers. The rear of the top will fold down automatically when it is folded. The smaller cut shows the top off and folded to one seat; the rear cushion and fall come out and can be set

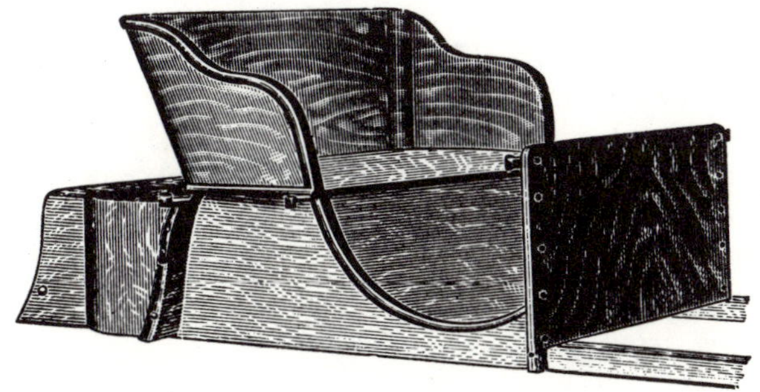

against the front fall, thus giving all the room in the body for luggage. It can be attached to bodies by taking them off. These bodies and tops are made by the Stratton Carriage Body Co., Muncie, Ind.

A Storm Front.

Apron or Storm Front for Touring Car.

The front piece was made to knob on first curve across inside of top and on dash at bottom, with a large light or transparent celluloid sewed in. This piece could be fitted tight up and down. The sides were knobbed on the inside of top rail down the side on inside of front post. The front piece and side pieces were buckled on sides, and a billet piece was put on front. The side pieces when not used should be taken off, rolled up and put away. On the front piece two buckles and straps were put on to roll up, and could be unknobbed and taken off if desired. To make this apron front, cut pieces the size desired. In the apron referred to the front piece was cut out of 50-inch goods, cutting off 4 feet of the goods for front piece.

The side pieces were cut 3 feet 6 inches; the depth of side pieces being more than the width of the goods it is necessary to piece the sides sewing 6 inches on bottom, making a lap seam, having pieces ready fit them on the job. Tack the goods on the curve and dash temporarily and then mark for knobs on curve and knob patches on the curtain. There should be enough knobs to hold tight at the top as there is quite a pull on the curtain when the auto is going fast. Eight knobs were used on this curtain across the top of the front, 5 across the dash at the bottom. Mark for light, which is

8 inches down from top; having done this, tack the side pieces temporarily and mark them for knobs and patches on the sides. Six knobs were put on inside the top rail and 5 down the inside of the front post on the front piece. When cutting allow enough goods to go around the sides about 6 inches, in order to form a flap, so that when the front and sides are buckled fast there will be lap enough to lay close together.

Then mark for buckles and straps, putting about 4 on each side. This would make them 7 inches apart on this apron, putting the buckle pieces on the sides and billet pieces on the front. The side pieces of course are longer than front as they must go down below the sill. Put two knob patches on side pieces below the buckles so that they will knob around on front about an inch and a half. a patch on front piece and side pieces taking the same knob at top of dash. The back part of the sides is knobbed on the inside

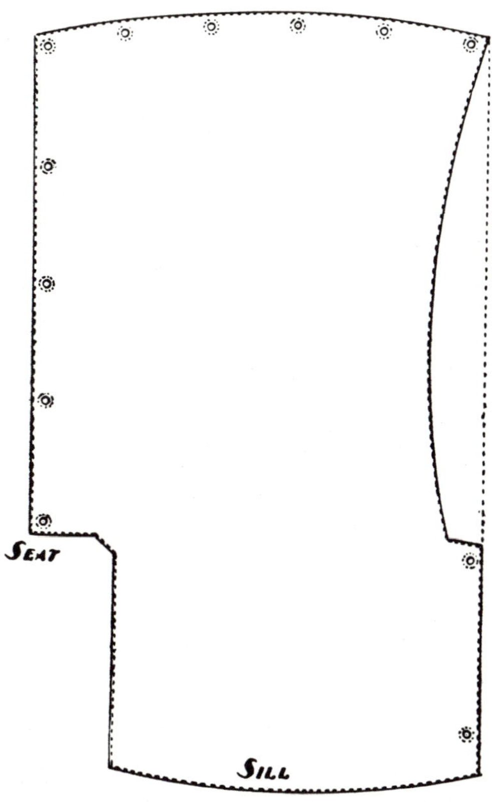

Side Curtain for Touring Car.

of the front post to make it handy to fasten on or take off from the inside. It is necessary to make a tuck about 6 or 8 inches to fit on the outside below the seat line. Mark for this. Cut where side pieces go around on front of dash below the top of the dash. Cut this 2½ inches and you now have all the marks that are needed. Take the goods off the job and make up; first make front pieces; cut goods so that they will fit snugly around the curve close to the top.

Cut down about ½ inch on each side for the top rail, then cut the sides with a sweep from bottom of side rail at top to top of dashboard at bottom. Allow it to sweep 6 inches in the center; this gives us our flap to go around the sides. Then cut the bottom; at each side allow the goods to go about 4 inches below the top of the dashboard; then cut with a sweep up from side to side. This sweep is necessary on the bottom on account of the shield that is on the front of most autos to cover the works. Then turn down a hem and sew on the sewing machine. First reinforce where the cuts were made in the corners of the top rail and at the top of the dash. When sewed up stitch on knob patches by hand, also billet straps on sides; these straps are ¾ inch wide and 5 inches long. The knob patches are 1½ inches long; and have patches and straps stitched on.

Then put in the light, which in the apron referred to is 2 feet 6 inches long, and 20 inches wide, and 8 inches below the curve. This light is a transparent piece of celluloid, and can be rolled up. To sew this light in, cut a space in the goods large enough allowing about 2 inches for turnunder. Lay the celluloid flap over the opening, take a piece of the same goods about 3 inches wide to go all around the light on the inside for binding. Baste this through to hold the celluloid and the goods in place while you are sewing fast. There should be 3 or 4 rows of stitching all around this light and the stitch should be pretty long, say 4 or 5 to the inch, as the celluloid is more or less brittle. The long stitch is better and should be used.

This front piece is made to knob and can be taken off. There is also provision made for rolling up. There is a long strap ¾ x 18 inches with a ¾-inch skate buckle riveted on. This is put on for rolling up. The strap is lapped around the top of the front about 2 inches on each end, and riveted through and through with a strap on one side and buckle on the other. When this front is used without the sides the piece which was allowed to go around the sides, or flap with straps on, would not look attractive and would flap in the wind. To overcome this put two buckles on

the inside of the front on each side. Use a ⅜ No. 10 rivet where
the binding is around the light, or inside, as the material is stitched
there and will hold. Put the buckle on to correspond with the
billet straps so that the flap can be folded over and the billet put
through the buckle, where it will be held fast in place.

This leaves enough space for the occupant to observe what is in
front and at the same time be protected from inclement weather.
The straps which hold the front in place when it is dropped, as
above stated, should be put on outside of the front so that it will
drop toward the inside. This front is a protection against wet
and cold weather.

THE SIDES.

The goods being cut and fitted, cut across the top with a little
sweep making them to fit up tight to the top the same as on the
front, and down the front with a sweep from the rail to the dashboard. Then straight down from the top of the dash to the sill on
the front of the piece. Cut straight down from the top rail along
the post to the seat. It is necessary to cut out along the seat line,
which on this job was 6 inches, and then down on the outside to the
bottom of the sill. When all is cut put the corner pieces in to
strengthen where the corners are and sew on the machine.

When sewed, stitch on the knob patches and buckle pieces by
hand, and the apron is complete. These knob patches are 1½-
inch with ¾-inch skate buckle. When the two sides and front
are done, put on the job, using No. 56 driving knobs for hanging
the apron on knob, the front pieces across the curve on top and
the dash at bottom. Knob the side pieces to the rail at the top
and down the front post on the inside. Then buckle front and
sides together at the front, when it is all closed in. A similar
storm front can also be used on a regular dash front delivery wagon.

Oiling Old Straps.

It is customary to oil all straps in a second-hand carriage when
it is done up and neats-foot oil is generally used. Its tendency is
to turn to a white appearance and it is therefore recommended to mix
a small amount of black paint with the oil before applying. This
will retain the blackness of the strap.

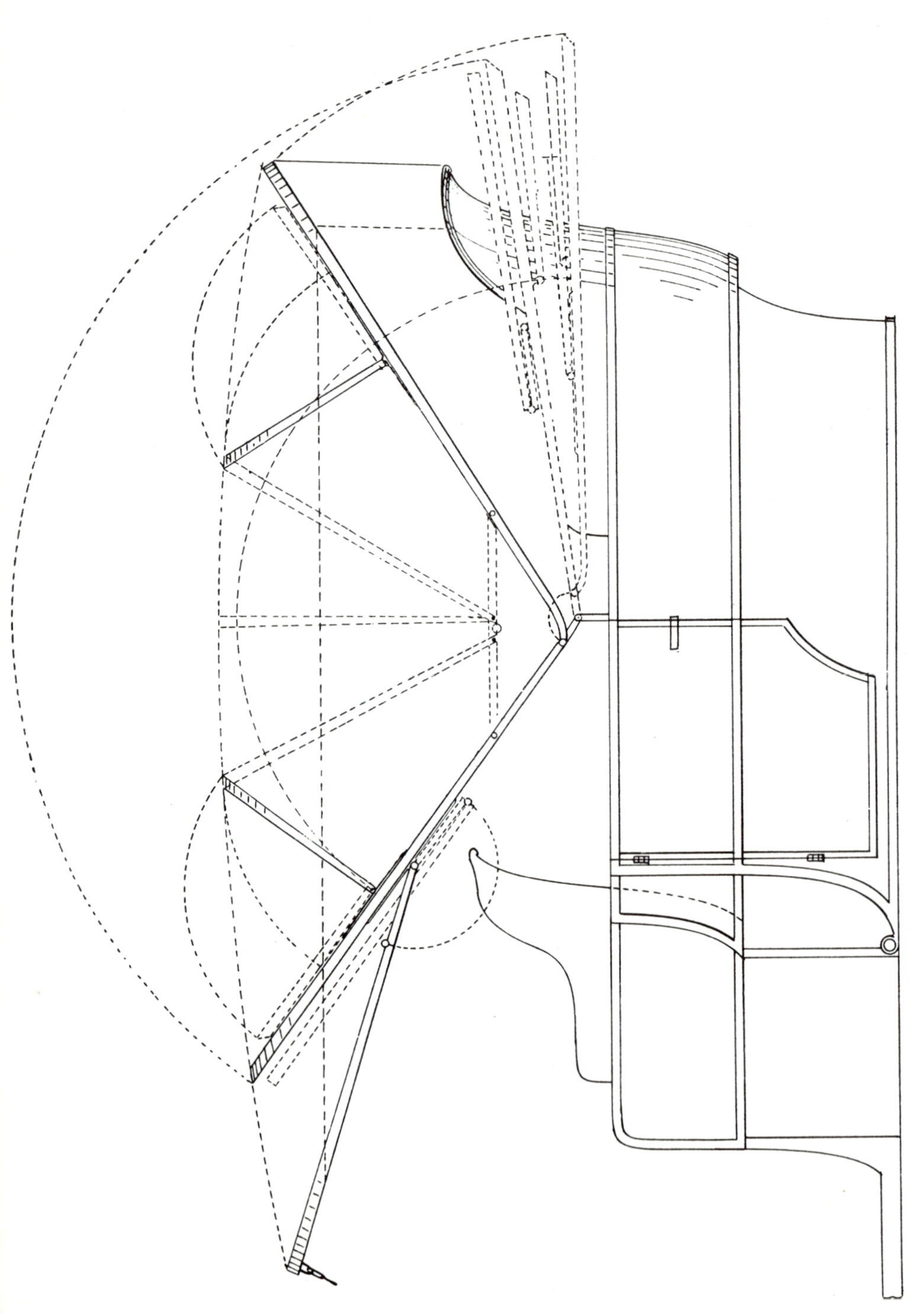

A Four-Bow, Closed Top, Side-Entrance, Touring Car.

The body on which this top is mounted is one of those well-designed and correctly built structures which has been admired and copied by builders in this country. We herewith furnish some of the dimensions which are necessary for the building of this style of top for such size of body.

The extreme length of this top is 5 feet 5 inches. The rear flare is ½ inch only, and is just enough to retain the vertical

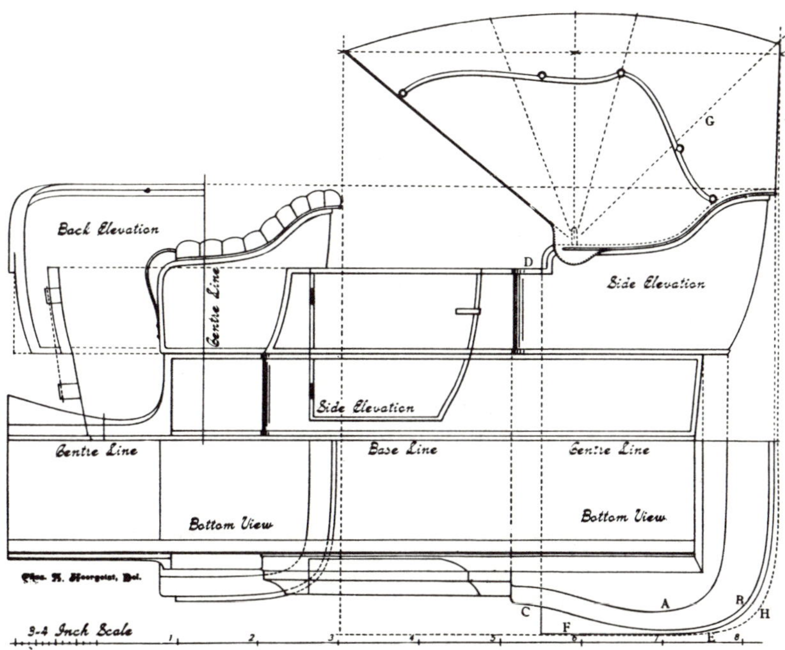

A four-bow, closed top, side-entrance, touring car.

appearance. The front height of top from the top of the seat is 44¼ inches, and the rear height from the seat is 45 inches, and at the center 49¾ inches. All of the dimensions are taken from the top of the seat, not the top of the cushion, to the outside of the top. The automobile cushions are generally spring cushions, and are 2 inches higher than carriage cushions, thus making the regular height as used for carriage tops at the center of the top. Note the front end of the top, which is on a plumb line with the back of the trimming on the front seat. The slant of the front bow is in proportion to its length, and the center of the slat iron is in the same position as on a carriage top. From this center the front part of the top is 3 inches longer than the rear of the top, thus showing the proportions of the top are the same as carriage tops, excepting their is less top curve.

Now note the width on the bottom view. Line A is the seat frame curve and B the false arm rail curve, which shows the shape of the seat top and on which the lower edge of the top is secured. C is the width on D, but the entire width of body on the false arm rail E and near the slat iron F is 61½ inches, showing that the false arm rail runs from E to F in a parallel direction with the base line. All of the bows are bent alike and all have the same width and curve on top, and must correspond with the curve of the false arm rail and rear bow when in the position of dotted line G.

If the curves of the bows are too round, they will throw line H toward the false arm rail and throw the bow inward on top. This would detract a great deal from the good proportions. If the bows have not sufficient curve, it will throw the top out of H, and this will not look well either. The fact is that the bows must be bent in proportion to the curve of the false arm rail. The bows are all of the same width as shown on dotted line F, because the top of seat on which the top leather is fastened is one width across to E, and then it turns around the curve. For this reason the bows cannot drop further than the top edge of seat. If the top is made with side curtains the bows are curved toward the outside, the prop is lowered and the bows drop below the top of seat.

A Five-Bow, Closed Top, Side-Entrance, Touring Car.

The length of this top is 4 feet 11 inches, and it has a ¾-inch flare in the rear. The extreme end of the front bow is about on a plumb line with the rear of the front seat on the false arm rail. The rear half starting from center of slat iron is 26 inches, and

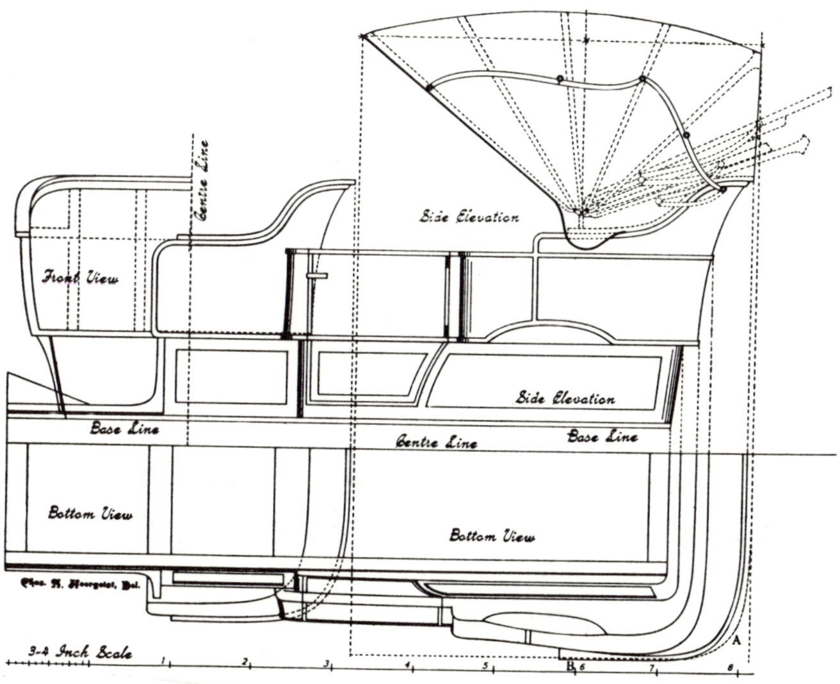

A five-bow, closed top, side-entrance, touring car.

the front half of the top from the center of the slat iron is 33 inches, showing a difference in length of 7 inches. In carriage top construction the difference is never more than 3 inches. In carriage construction the front is always lower and the rear end higher, while on this auto top the front bow is 1⅝ inches higher on the front than the rear bow. In all cases the front bow is generally plumb with the rear of the front seat. The height of the top from the top of the seat to the top of the center bow is 5 feet, which creates a nice curve from front to back of bow. If the front bow would be dropped as a carriage top, it would lessen the head room on entering the body, consequently such tops have been designed to answer the requirements of automobiles under existing conditions.

The four-bow top has a great advantage over the five-bow top. This top is not quite 5 feet long and has five bows, while other tops are made from 5 feet 6 to 7 inches, and have four bows only. As a matter of fact the outside width of bows is the same as the outside width of body, the same as on a cabriolet, but the cabriolet bodies are contracted and the bows drop over it. On such an auto top with auto seats as built at present, this cannot be done, and consequently the rear bow rests on top of the seat instead of on the prop iron on a cabriolet. This raises the front bow when down almost up to an angle of 45 degrees, which does not look well, consequently the four-bow top makes a better proportioned top.

This body is 61¼ inches wide from out to out of false arm rails, therefore the bows are 61 inches wide from out to out. The top curve of the bows when in position with top up must conform with the dotted line A, and the false arm rail must extend outward, as shown on B. These bodies are built for a 33½-inch wide chassis. Its rockers extend over the chassis 1 inch on each side. There is a recess of 1½ inches each side and a flare of 2½ inches for the body, making the top of the body under the seat 43½ inches wide. The top joints are double and all curved.

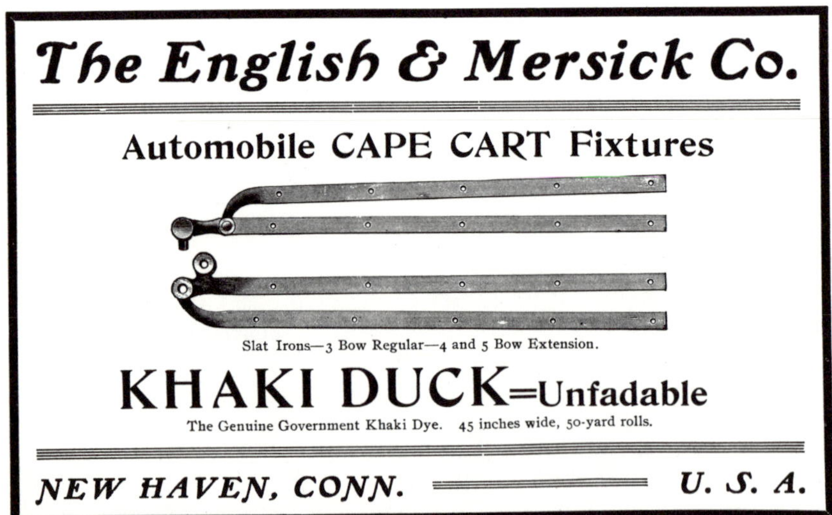

FITTING A CANOPY HEAD

The methods of fitting up open-bodied motors is becoming as varied as the design of the cars themselves. Though one would think that there was not much originality to be had in fitting canopy heads up, yet it is a branch of equipment in these carriages that calls for special handling and this is so much the case that no two manufacturers make their canopies alike in the mechanism of the fittings, though they are all in their own individual way, working to an effective but light head covering, which must harmonize with the character and design of the car it is fitted to.

The design of open car shown in accompanying illustration is of a plain yet sharp style and in character with those prevailing at present, but does not follow in the footsteps of the purloiner and copyist, who is ever ready to seize upon matter which he can misappropriate to his own uses without the fear of being legally called to answer for his conduct.

The seats or top quarters of the body are framed and paneled. The boot or sides of the body are of ⅞ in. stuff, and the bottomsides framed into them. The body is easily built and would look smart because of the sharp and clean cut of its lines.

The canopy head is fitted up to leave the spaces of getting in and out of the body as clear of impediment as the design will allow. The back slats are fixed to obtain a free clearance into the hind body. The front slat is made upright and fitted to a boss stay which is a permanent fixture to the body. To the slat iron is forged a projecting arm, A, to which the irons of the two hind slats are hinged and the slats cut off to line with the curve of the roof. The front slat is also fixed in an upright position, and the horizontal slat, B, is fixed to a plate joint at C. The plate at C goes right around the slat to keep it strong and to prevent it breaking away from its bent shape.

To the horizontal slat is fixed two roof slats of the same curve to line with the rise of the roof at D and E. The strap F is fixed at each side of the chassis. A short roof strap is fixed to the front slat, D, to which the long strap, F, is buckled, so that when the waterproofing is fitted and fixed to the slats, the straps are buckled up tight and the canopy held in position.

It will be as well to point out here that these heads are fixed much in the same way that a victoria hood slats are spaced and fixed to position with webbing. The position of the slats are first decided on and held in their spacings with ordinary webbing, used for such work in victoria and landau heads when the head cloth is being put in. Then the waterproofing is cut out to the required sizes and curves and welted around the seaming, and also hem-welted along the bottom line edges and down the corner curve of the back at G and H. The covering is fixed to the front horizontal slat and to the sides of the back slats and along the top rail of the hind quarter with eyelets and knobs. This style of canopy looks very smart, while it is light and airy and affords good protection from dust and weather.

Bow Sockets—

with C. F. Co's non-breakable back bow construction are endorsed by manufacturers, dealers and users. Send for Booklet "About Bow Sockets."

CORTLAND FORGING CO.,
CORTLAND, N. Y.

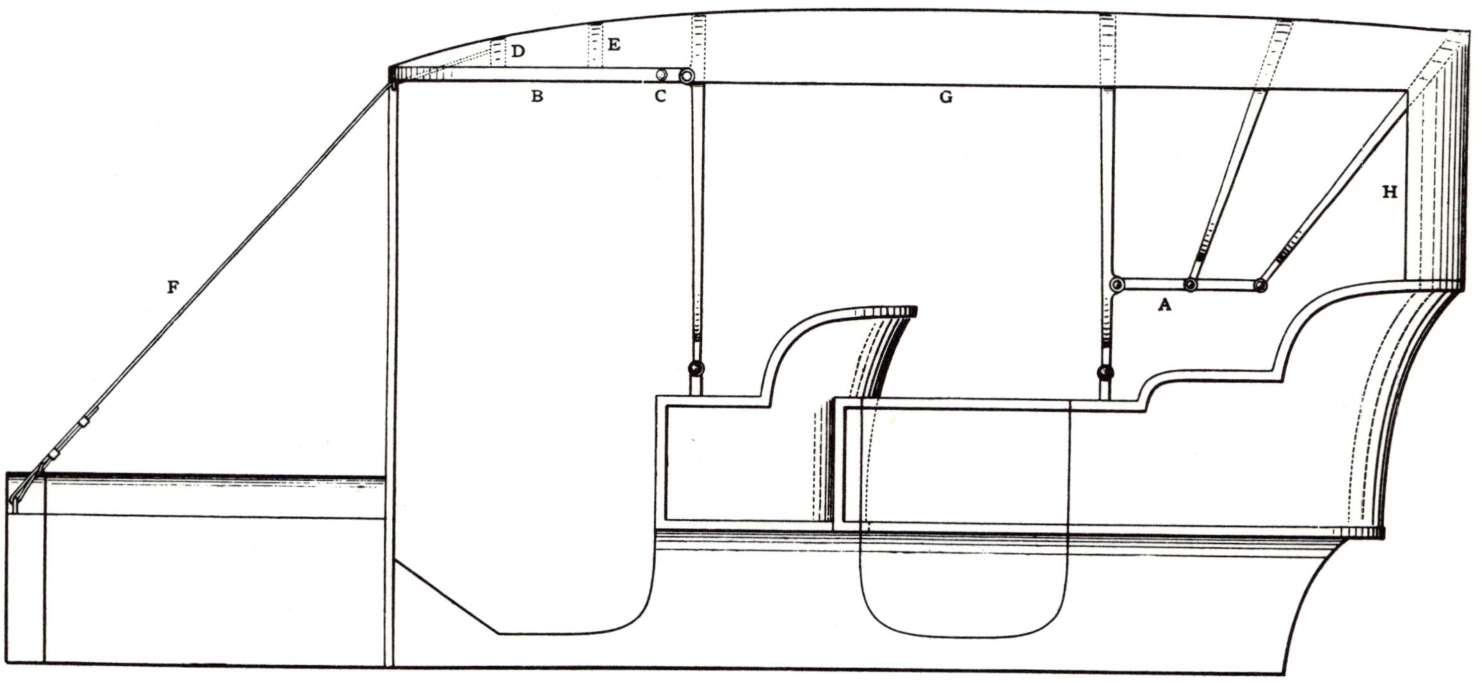

Fitting a Canopy Head to An Open-Bodied Car.

To Trim a Top for Three-Seat Motor Wagon

First, get the height from bottom of seat to the top of seat irons by placing a straight edge across seat and measuring from bottom of seat to straight edge, which will be 7½ inches. This will be the same on both front and rear seats. Then lay out the secondary or top bow irons. These are made up of ¾-inch iron to fit in the lower eyes above the seat sides; the space between the eyes is 13 inches apart. The iron for front seat has an eye 3 inches up from bottom of rail, and 4 inches from back, and with ⁷⁄₁₆-inch hole to take front bows when the top is folded, allowing it to extend out ¾ inch on each side. For this iron, measurement must be taken on inside, as the pins of front bow socket are on that side.

On the rear seat the iron is the same as front with exception of the goose neck, which is 3 inches from front eye of same seat and 3 inches high, and flares out ¾ inch. The width across the seats is 47½ inches with ¾-inch flare out of top iron on each side, which makes a total of 49 inches across seats. Using 50-inch wood bows, this allows 1 inch draw, that is ½ inch on each side.

The back seat iron for top has a bow rest for top when it is thrown back. This is made even with the back of seat and curved out 3 inches, made round to fit bow rest. Having got out your top iron, you next draft the top, which is 45½ inches high from bottom of seat, and extends 3¾ inches over the dash board. That makes the top 10 feet long. From back of rear seat to top iron it is 18 inches, giving 3½ plumb back. This makes the space 21½ inches from back bow to the fourth bow; between the irons of back and front seats is 56¼ inches. For the fourth bow use a handy shifting bow. The eye for bow is placed 14½ inches up from center of eye on fourth bow, using a clamp which is made specially for handy shifting bows.

The back bow has a 4-inch drop from the original height of top, which is 45½ inches. The handy shifting bow on back half of top is placed 30 inches front of fourth bow, numbering the bows from front to back; the second bow has ½-inch drop, and on this you also fasten a handy shifting bow socket. The clamps are placed 14½ inches, giving 3½ plumb back. This makes the space 21½ inches from from second bow, and has 6½ inches drop from the original height (45½ inches), thus allowing the top to extend 3¼ inches over the dash. The side valance is 12½ inches deep.

The seam on side valance and roof is 4½ inches in from outside of bow; this makes the roof piece 41 inches wide, also adding on

Showing the Trimming on a Three-Seat Extension Top Motor Wagon.

¾ inch on each side for turning under for seam, making the total width of 42½ inches. Measurement of bow sockets is taken from center of base, back 30 inches. Fourth bow is 24 inches long; handy shifting 28 inches long; front second is 24 inches, and front handy shifting 28 inches long.

Having the top drafted and bows driven in the bow sockets, using japanned sockets which for good service are considered better than the leather covered sockets for this style of a car. Now cover the wood bows with bow covering to match the inside of fabric used for top. Cut the covering the width of the goods, piecing it on the round of the bows. By doing this you save material, but if you have plenty of material cut it out of the goods on the bias, 5¼ inches wide, as this will suit the average bows.

Bows being covered place them on the top horse, setting them to correspond with the irons on body, which will be 56¼ inches between bows. As you are using 50-inch bows for the top, adjust the horse to measure 48 inches across; this will give the same position of top as when on the body. Screw the slat irons to the bow. The holes in these irons can be drilled every ½ inch apart, thus making them to fit almost any size top. Place irons so the top of them will be on a line for bottom of the side valance or quarter.

You then tack on the stretchers, placing one lengthwise of top in center, then from left to right lengthwise. Then cut out the pads, which are usually 11 inches. Crease down ½ inch on each side, which makes up when finished 10 inches.

The marks on the bows for side valance are 12½ inches down from top of bows. Cut the valance to go 2½ inches over seam mark on bows, 3 inches to turn-under for dusters, marking ¾ inch on each end. This is done to give bottom of valance a sweep when put in place. It will be straight on bottom, and this will make the valance cut-out ready to make up, to measure 18 inches. Cut out a strip for the duster 3½ inches wide the length of the side valance; crease down ½ inch on each side and sew up one side. The other side can be sewed when you are making up the valance.

Th back stays are cut 7¾ inches at the bottom, curved up so it will meet the side valance around on side of bows. This will make about 15 inches at top of stay when stays are in place.

Make the back curtain to overlap each stay 2¼ inches, placing the curtain fasteners 1⅛ inches in from sides. This top has four curtains on each side and a storm front curtain. These curtains can be made out of single texture fabric same as the top. Back curtains and back stays are of double texture. The material used for a top of this kind is 16¾ yards of top fabric. Imitation leather is the best material for a top for this kind of a car.

There are required 1¼ yards bow covering, 13⅔ yards strain webbing, 2½ sheets of celluloid, 20 x 50 inches (large sheets); one pair back stay straps; one pair top straps, 50 inches long; 3½ pounds of hair for pads; 3 papers 4-ounce tacks; one paper saddle nails (10-ounce); ¼ paper 12-ounce tacks for stays and straps; 2 roll-up straps; 2 drive knobs; 56 curtain fasteners; 1 yard buckram for back stays; 3½ yards top padding; 1 paper 2½-ounce tacks; ½ pound paste for stays; 1 spool thread for sewing machine; ¾ gross brass screws for fasteners, ⅝-inch, No. 6 flat head; 1 pair bow rests and straps; 8 steel screws, 1-inch No. 8 for back stay straps and top straps; 1 set of 4-bow japanned handy shifting sockets, and 2 extra handy shifting sockets for back half of top.

The backs are made up with springs bridled down until they are 3 inches high, fitting a piece of No. 10 sail duck across springs. This will be a pattern for the back, which is made up half diamond at top and biscuit at bottom. Blocks are laid out with ten buttons across, 4¼ inches apart. The first row of buttons is 4½ inches from bottom of seat; next is 9 inches, and the point of diamond is 3¼ inches. Top is 4 inches down from top of back. On the lower rows of buttons allow 1½ inches from buttons down to bottom with ¼-inch fullness at point of diamond. A·ross bottom allow ¾-inch fullness. This back will take 37 buttons. The cushions are made in biscuit design, 4 x 4¾ inches, with falls attached to cushion.

The material used for body is: Two hides of leather of 56 inches each or 9 yds. imitation leather; 24 back springs; 3 woven springs for 3 cushions; 18 pounds hair; 2 gross buttons; 4 yards sail duck, 50 inches wide for cushion and backs; 3 pieces soft dash leather for facings on front of cushions; 2 papers·4-ounce tacks; 1 paper 2½-ounce tacks; 2½ pounds paste; 1 spool thread; 1 paper gimp tacks.

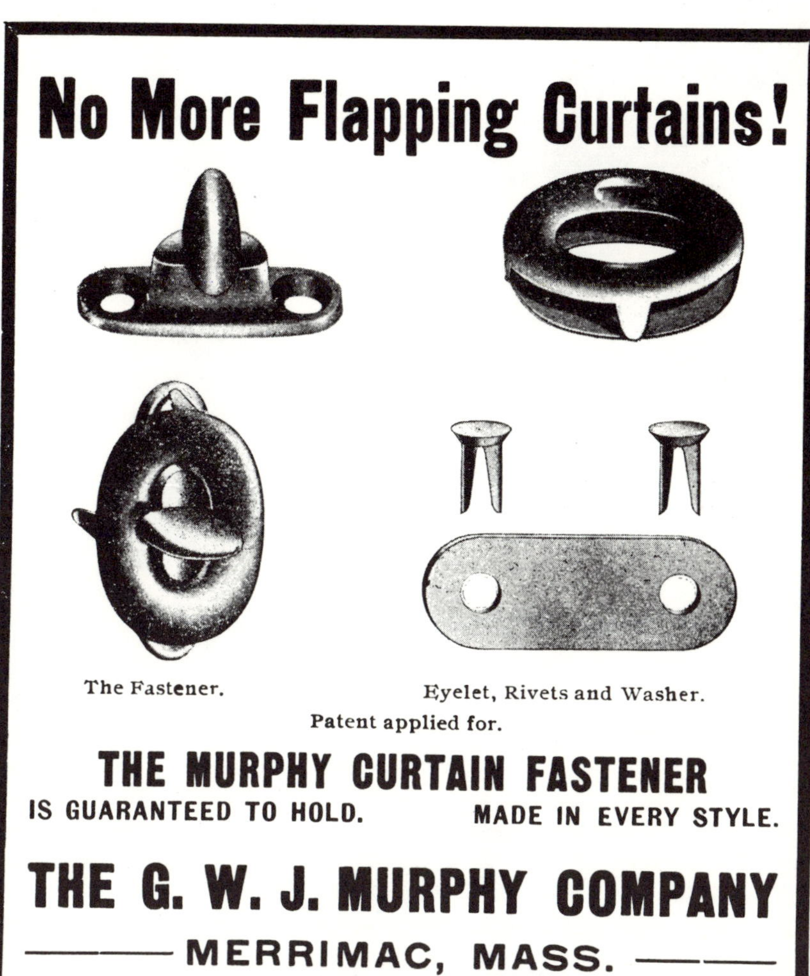

"TAILOR-MADE AUTO TOPS AT A SAVING OF ONE-THIRD TO ONE-HALF

Four-Bow Extension Touring Car Tops

Touring Car Top with Joint Side Irons

For such cars as *Cadillac 30, Buick Model 10 Touring Car, E. M. F., Mora Model "I," Ford Model, Chalmers Detroit Model "F," White Steamer Model "O," Maxwell 2 and 4 Cylinder Touring Cars, Overland, Franklin, Stevens-Duryea, etc.*

We present herewith a line of tops at prices positively beyond duplication; from the least expensive to the highest grade; they embody all the finest workmanship and material that was ever put into an auto top at any price. The designs are such that will appeal to the discriminating motorist. The great saving will appeal to those who are seeking the best the market affords at prices that cannot be duplicated elsewhere. Made complete with irons to attach to socket iron on body, including side curtains, with large celluloid lights. Heavy second growth ash bows, with extra bow sockets, japanned or leather covered as ordered, with brass bow separators. Top lined or unlined, as ordered. Bows nicely covered overhead on unlined tops nicely padded over bows, made with joint side irons as illustrated, or with front and rear strainer straps, as ordered; has drop prop rests to allow top to clash well back; brass or black half-turn knobs throughout, brass or black prop nuts, brass or black fasteners in side quarters between bows to hold side curtains.

PLEASE NOTE: When not otherwise specified, these tops will be made with joint side irons with leather covered bows and without storm fronts.

The following prices apply to all runabouts not larger than any of the above cars already enumerated (note our extraordinary low prices):

FOUR-BOW EXTENSION TOURING CAR TOPS

With Japanned Bow Sockets Without Storm Front

Cat. No.	Material	Reg. Price	Cut Price
201	Fairfield rubber, 24 oz. green back	$69.50	**$41.50**
202	Fairfield Rubber, 24 oz. red back	69.50	**41.50**
205	Fairfield Rubber, 36 oz. green back	72.00	**47.25**
210	Black Fabrikoid, Imitation Leather	74.50	**44.25**
211	Red Fabrikoid, Imitation Leather	75.50	**45.00**
213	Russet Fabrikoid, Imitation Leather	75.50	**45.00**
216	Whipcord Mackintosh	80.50	**47.75**
217	Plain Dark Mackintosh	80.50	**47.75**
219	Imitation Pantasote	80.50	**47.75**
222	Black Pantasote, black back	96.00	**57.00**
223	Black Pantasote, whipcord back	102.00	**60.00**
225	Black Pantasote, red back	102.00	**60.00**
227	Red Pantasote, red back	102.00	**60.00**
228	Russet Pantasote, whipcord back	102.00	**60.00**
231	English Khaki, dark	106.75	**63.50**
233	Mohair Cravenette	106.75	**63.50**

FOUR-BOW EXTENSION TOURING CAR TOPS

With Leather-Covered Bow Sockets Without Storm Front

Cat. No.	Material	Reg. Price	Cut Price
201	Fairfield rubber, 24 oz. green back	$75.50	**$45.00**
202	Fairfield Rubber, 24 oz. red back	75.50	**45.00**
205	Fairfield Rubber, 36 oz. green back	69.25	**46.25**
210	Black Fabrikoid, Imitation Leather	80.50	**47.75**
211	Red Fabrikoid, Imitation Leather	81.50	**48.50**
213	Russet Fabrikoid, Imitation Leather	81.50	**48.50**
216	Whipcord Mackintosh	86.50	**51.25**
217	Plain Dark Mackintosh	86.50	**51.25**
219	Imitation Pantasote	86.50	**51.25**
222	Black Pantasote, black back	102.00	**60.00**
223	Black Pantasote, whipcord back	108.00	**64.25**
225	Black Pantasote, red back	108.00	**64.25**
227	Red Pantasote, red back	108.00	**64.25**
228	Russet Pantasote, whipcord back	108.00	**64.25**
231	English Khaki, dark	112.75	**67.00**
233	Mohair Cravenette	112.75	**67.00**

The above prices are quoted without any storm fronts, unlined. We will furnish storm fronts at the following prices:

THREE-PIECE STORM FRONT AND SIDES

(Reaches Clear Around to Side Curtains and Encloses Top Completely)

Cat. Nos.	Cut Price
201, 202	**$9.00**
205, 210, 211, 213	**9.50**
216, 217	**11.00**
219, 222, 223, 225	**14.00**
227, 228, 231, 233	**15.00**

ONE-PIECE STORM FRONT

(Extends Only the Width of the Dash)

Cat. Nos.	Cut Price
201, 202	**$5.00**
205, 210, 211, 213	**5.50**
216, 217	**5.75**
219, 222, 223, 225	**7.25**
227, 228, 231, 233	**8.00**

EXTRAS: For lining, except side curtains, with 9 oz. all-wool green or red broadcloth or whipcord, $8.50. For lining, except side curtains, with 16 oz. all-wool green or blue broadcloth or whipcord, $16.00. For brass finish across front bow, $2.00; brass finish across back bow, $2.00; brass plated joints, $4.00; brass plated iron attached to irons on body, $2.50. Long wood bows, natural finish and brass plated slat irons, $6.50.

You Are Not Getting Your Money's Worth If You Pay More Than We Ask

"TAILOR-MADE" AUTO TOPS AT A SAVING OF ONE-THIRD TO ONE-HALF

Three-Bow Runabout Tops

For such runabouts as *Maxwell, Ford, Buick, Reo, Overland, E. M. F., Chalmers, Detroit, Cadillac Franklin, Stevens-Duryea,* etc.

Runabout Top with Joint Side Irons

Made complete, ready to bolt on car to irons, including side curtains, with large celluloid lights, with or without storm front, as ordered, heavy second growth ash bows with strong bow sockets, japanned or leather covered, as ordered, with brass bow separators, with tops lined or unlined, as ordered; bows nicely covered overhead on unlined tops, nicely padded over bows, made with joint side irons (curved or straight) as illustrated, or with front and rear strainer straps, as ordered; has drop prop rests to allow top to clash well back; brass or black half-turn knobs throughout, brass or black prop nuts, brass or black fasteners in side quarters between bows to hold side curtains.

PLEASE NOTE: When not otherwise specified, tops of this style will be made unlined, with joint side irons, with japanned bow sockets, and without storm front.

The following prices apply to all runabouts not larger than any of the above cars already enumerated (note our extraordinary low prices):

| DIRECTIONS FOR ORDERING |

Please give make, model and year of your car, and state distinctly whether you want japanned or leather covered bows; whether joint irons or strainer straps; if with or without storm front; three-piece or one-piece. Three-piece storm front reaches clear around to side curtain and encloses top completely; while one-piece storm front extends only the width of the dash. While we have the measurements on our files of all popular makes of cars, it will assist us materially to fill your orders promptly if all the above-required information is given. *Sample Card of Materials furnished free of charge upon request.*

THREE-BOW RUNABOUT TOPS
With Japanned Bow Sockets Without Storm Front

Cat. No.	Material	Reg. Price	Cut Price
101	Fairfield Rubber, 24 oz. green back	$36.00	**$21.50**
102	Fairfield Rubber, 24 oz. red back	36.00	**21.50**
105	Fairfield Rubber, 36 oz. green back	38.00	**23.75**
110	Black Fabrikoid, Imitation Leather	39.50	**24.50**
111	Red Fabrikoid, Imitation Leather	40.25	**25.75**
113	Russet Fabrikoid, Imitation Leather	40.25	**26.50**
116	Whipcord Mackintosh	42.00	**27.50**
117	Plain Dark Mackintosh	42.00	**27.50**
119	Imitation Pantasote	42.00	**27.50**
122	Black Pantasote, black back	42.00	**28.50**
123	Black Pantasote, whipcord back	50.50	**29.00**
125	Black Pantasote, red back	50.50	**29.00**
127	Red Pantasote, red back	50.50	**29.00**
128	Russett Pantasote, whipcord back	50.50	**29.00**
131	English Khaki, dark	52.75	**31.25**
133	Mohair Cravenette	52.75	**31.25**

THREE-BOW RUNABOUT TOPS
With Leather-Covered Bow Sockets Without Storm Front

Cat. No.	Material	Reg. Price	Cut Price
101	Fairfield Rubber, 24 oz. green back	$42.00	**$23.75**
102	Fairfield Rubber, 24 oz. red back	42.00	**23.75**
105	Fairfield Rubber, 36 oz. green back	45.00	**26.75**
110	Black Fabrikoid, Imitation Leather	46.75	**27.50**
111	Red Fabrikoid, Imitation Leather	48.00	**28.50**
113	Russet Fabrikoid, Imitation Leather	48.00	**28.50**
116	Whipcord Mackintosh	51.50	**31.00**
117	Plain Dark Mackintosh	51.50	**31.00**
119	Imitation Pantasote	51.50	**31.00**
122	Black Pantasote, black back	57.50	**31.50**
123	Black Pantasote, whipcord back	60.00	**33.00**
125	Black Pantasote, red back	60.00	**33.00**
127	Red Pantasote, red back	60.00	**33.00**
128	Russett Pantasote, whipcord back	60.00	**33.00**
131	English Khaki, dark	63.00	**34.50**
133	Mohair Cravenette	63.00	**34.50**

The above prices are quoted without any storm fronts, unlined. We will furnish storm fronts at the following prices:

THREE-PIECE STORM FRONT AND SIDES
(Reaches Clear Around to Side Curtains and Enclose)

Cat. No.	Cut Price
101, 102	**$9.00**
105, 110, 111, 113	**9.25**
116, 117	**11.00**
119, 122, 123, 125	**13.75**
127, 128, 131, 133	**15.25**

ONE-PIECE STORM FRONT
(Extends Only the Width of the Dash)

Cat. No.	Cut Price
101, 102	**$5.00**
105, 110, 111, 113	**5.25**
116, 117	**5.50**
119, 122, 123, 125	**7.00**
127, 128, 131, 133	**7.50**

EXTRAS: For lining, except side curtains, with 16 oz. all-wool green or red broadcloth or whipcord, add $3.25; for lining, including side curtain, with 6 oz. all-wool green or red broadcloth or whipcord, add $5.00; for lining, except side curtain, with 10 oz. all-wool green or red broadcloth or whipcord, add $5.00; for lining, including side curtain, with 10 oz. all-wool green or red broadcloth or whipcord, add $7.50. Six joints instead of four joints, add $1.25. For long wood bows, natural finish and brass plated slat irons, add $2.50; for brass joints instead of black, add $3.00.

Light Three-Bow Top for Commercial Cars

On commercial cars that have no top over the entire body there are different styles of storm tops to protect the chauffeur and different methods of covering them.

The small cape top such as is used on a runabout is generally employed, and, although heavy bows and bow sockets are used, these tops will not last long on this kind of work on account of the rough usage they are subjected to. We give a description of a style of top for this class of work, which, while not as expensive as a cape top, will be stronger and will give better service and at the same time, when properly made, will look well.

The top that we will describe is made much the same as a regular three-bow top, such as is used on regular wagon work, except that the arrangement of the bows is a little different and the top irons are placed back further on the seat than on a regular wagon so as not to interfere with the working of the levers or steering wheel, and the front bow is placed up high on center bow, so as to make easy access for the driver of the car.

Making Top

The woodworker, of course, first makes the top, using a good, heavy bow and heavy seat irons, making the bows and seat irons the same as on a regular wagon storm top, except that the seat irons are placed farther back on an automobile seat than on a wagon seat, placing them in the middle or a little back of middle of seat, so that the driver is able to work the steering gear and levers without coming in contact with the bow. Then the front bow is riveted to middle bow, about three-quarters way up, so as to make easy access for driver. There is a joint bolted on front and back bows on inside to hold bows apart same as on a regular storm top, and a hook fastened to back of seat with an eyebolt on middle bow, which holds the top in place. When this work is done the top is ready to be trimmed.

Trimming Top

To trim this top for the commercial automobile, either white or black duck could be used, but white duck is generally preferred, using No. 6 duck. First measure the width of seat, then the distance from back of seat to seat iron, then the distance from seat iron to front of seat, the height of iron above seat panel and depth of seat panel. When you have the correct measurements, set up the stand upon which these tops are generally made and mark the middle of front and back bows; tack a strip of goods across each side of top,

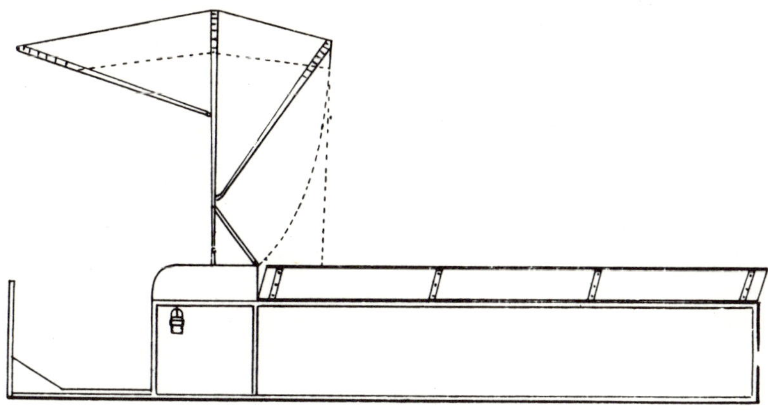

Light Three-Bow Top for Commercial Cars.

tacking on front and back bows, then space top off correctly so that front bow will about set over the dash and back bow will set over the back of seat, and when bows are spaced as near right as possible tack the strips fast to middle bow. These strips hold the bows in place while the top is being trimmed and are ripped off when top is done.

When top is ready measure for the top piece, allowing this to extend down on side about six inches, using the width of duck that suits best. Then place top piece on bows, tacking temporarily and working out smooth; then tack fast around the front of front bow, using six-ounce lining nails, leaving loose three inches up on sides; then tack fast on middle bow except a few inches at bottom.

When the top is in place the curtains are fitted on job, using the width of goods that cuts to the best advantage. First fit on the side curtains, allowing them to go around six inches on back. When sides are tacked on temporarily, mark sides, making a small mark at each tack mark for a screw-eye on bow and a screw-eye or strap at bottom of seat, whichever works to the best advantage. Cut a piece and fit on for the back curtain, tacking on bow and at the bottom mark at tacks on bow and mark for three fasteners at the bottom of curtain, using either straps or screw-eyes, the straps being the best if they can be used, making the side and back curtains take the same fastener. Mark half way up on curtain for a strap on back curtain to take a buckle on side curtain; then mark around on inside, marking down front bows, around top of seat panel, and where top and sides are to be joined together. When all marked, take curtains off job and make up.

Making Up Curtains

To make up curtains cut two inches out from marks at bow and two inches out from front of seat and cut with a sweep from top to bottom of curtain. The large piece that is cut out is used for a lining piece around back corners of side curtains. Then cut two inches from marks at top of curtains, which allows for a large lap where top and sides are joined together. Cut at bottom of curtains enough to allow curtain to finish one inch above bottom of seat panel. Then when all the parts are cut the curtains are creased down, using a double hem where there is a raw edge and a single hem where there is a selvage. When the hem is creased down, baste in the piece that you have cut out of front of curtain, basting this piece in at bottom of side curtains, placing the wide side of piece towards the back of curtain so that curtain is double thick at back corners of seat. When these lining pieces are basted in place the curtains are sewed on machine and the fasteners put in.

The best fasteners to use on these tops are straps riveted to curtains and a buckle tacked to the body and one screw-eye on the middle of each front bow. The straps are one inch wide, eight inches long, riveted on bottom of curtains to take a one-inch skate buckle tacked on body.

There should be two straps on each side curtain, one at each end, and three straps on back curtain, the end straps on back curtain to take the same buckle as strap on side curtain. When the straps are all riveted on curtains, place a curtain light in back curtain about nine inches down from bow and curtains are ready to be placed on top.

To place curtains on the job first make eight roll-up straps and tack on bows, four for the back curtain and two on each side curtain. Then find the tack holes in curtains to correspond with tack holes in bows, made while fitting curtains, and tack temporarily. When curtains are hung right, tack fast, using four-ounce tacks. Then pull top piece over smooth, turn under and tack fast across top of back bow, using six-ounce lining nails one inch apart. When all tacked fast the top piece and side curtains are sewed together, making two rows of stitching, using a heavy white sail twine. When top and sides are sewed together the knobs are driven in for the roll-up straps and top is complete. Take top off frame, place on job, putting top on seat irons; screw nuts tight and tack the buckles in place on the body and top is done.

CABRIOLET HOOD

IT is easily apparent to the bodymaker that exactitude is necessary in the marking in, setting out, also letting in the various hinges and joints, if the hood is to work sweetly, stand square and true, and when the hood is locked all joints must be up square, with the necessary clearance for paint and varnish, and also it must work freely in closing up " concertina " fashion. This particular hood is probably one of the simplest, and the various parts are enumerated in Plates XXI to XXVI. In the place of the ordinary pillar hinge, we have a specially made joint, keeping the centre low, the cranked elbow that carries the pillar joint being made out of $\frac{9}{16}$ in. round, and being exposed, this fitting is " brassed " all over.

The top cant rail hinge is placed in the ordinary manner—with stout $1\frac{1}{4}$ in. brass butts let in, and the same to the rear stretcher bar (No. 2, Plate XXII). These front bars are made out of birch or mahogany. The ordinary $\frac{1}{2}$ in. knuckle joints are to be used, and the hinging of the extremity of each end with its flaps is seen. Nos. 3, 4, and 5 are the ordinary hoopsticks bent with a corner at the back to welt the leather. Carefully let in the hinges, fixing the same temporarily with small screws, testing that all work is square to the joints both upwards and sideways, likewise when the hood is folded. See that the cant rails are also quite square with the pillars when all is extended. This is essential to a good job.

We have outside head joints, but to make a clean job the pillar tops and the under sides of the top half have brass " polished " plates fixed. In this hood the leather or other covering is not fixed to the cant rail along the hoopsticks, but brought over the rail and welted. The front light pillars are cut off and hinged to fold as usual and connected with the cant rail with a pillar fastener, a drop or folding light or screen being fitted to work behind driver's seat.

A Sectional Drawing of a Cabriolet Body showing Folding Hood and Fittings.—It will be seen (Plate XXII) that the hind door pillar top is hinged by an off-set lug, pivoted and connected to a lug on body, both to take the weight of the parts, and to assist in the lifting and opening out of the hood. The usual telescopic spring is used, the upper end, jointed to top part of pillar, and the lower end to the body, behind the hinge. The

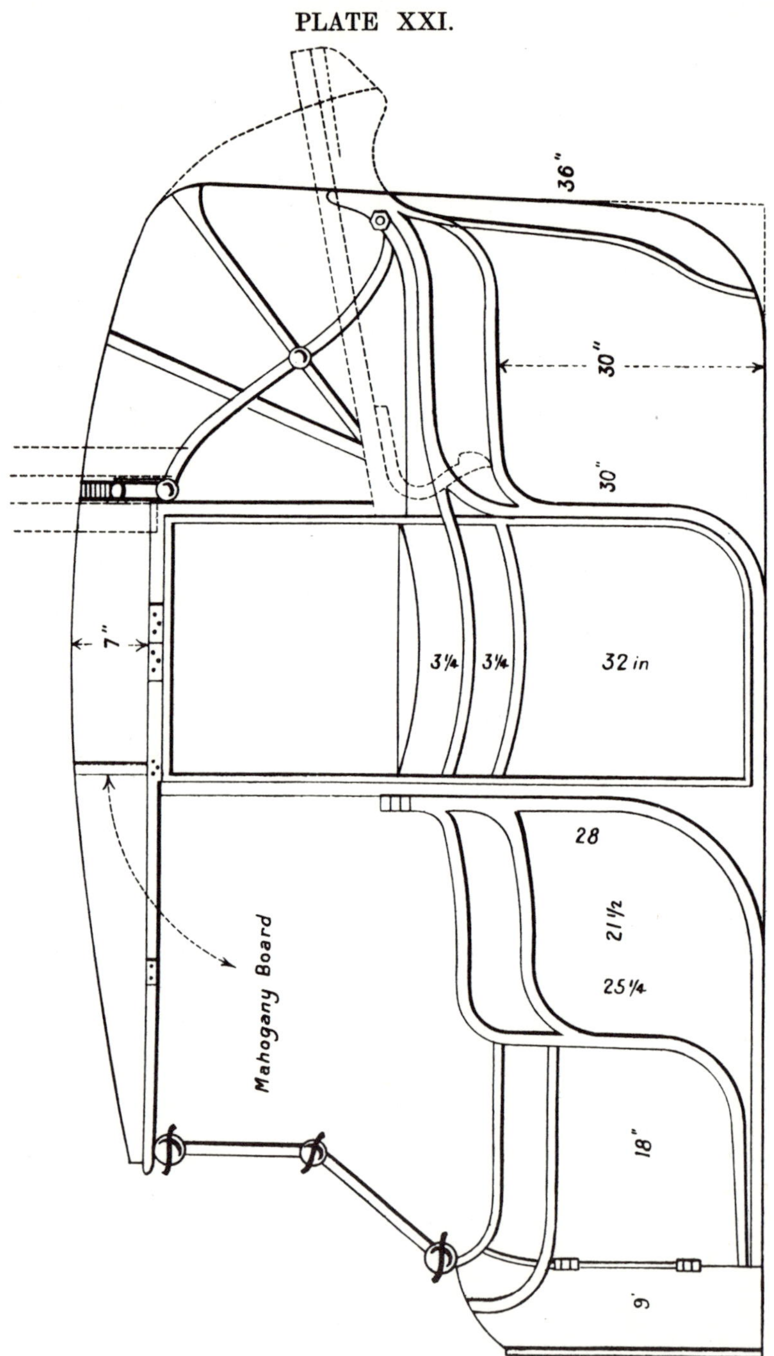
36"
30"
30"
7"
3¼
3¼
32 in
28
21½
25¼
18"
9'
Mahogany Board

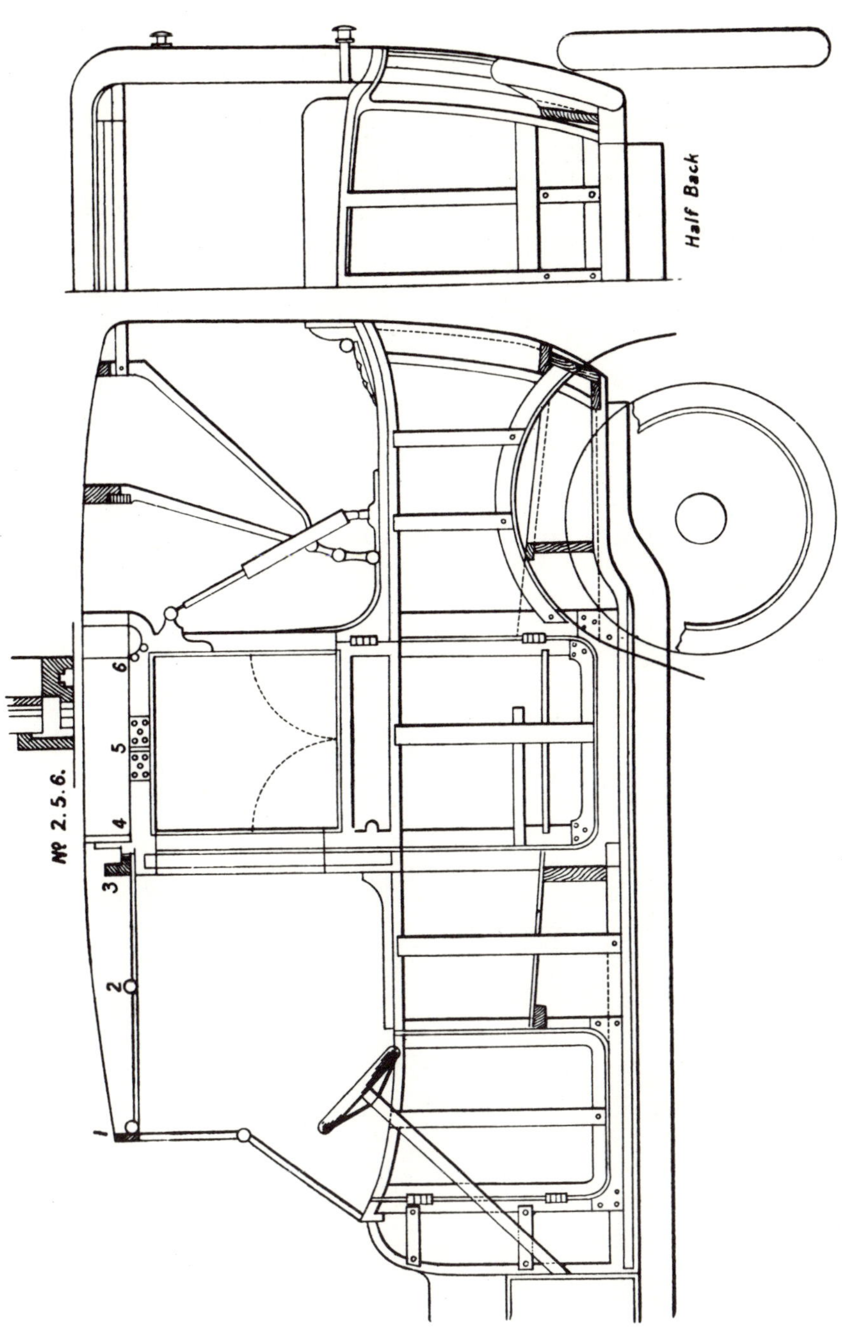
Half Back
№ 2.5.6.
1
2
3
4
5
6

usual neck plates carry the hoopsticks. The cant rail has its rear end abutting against the pillar, while in front it rests on the inwardly folding front pillars. The rail is connected to the hind standing pillar, by means of two links, which are arranged substantially, and horizontally, and jointed to the side of the cant rail at a point considerably forward, while the other end is arranged nearly vertical and has its upper extremity jointed to the inner end of the cant rail. To ensure a simultaneous folding of the parts a normally vertically disposed radius link is employed on the pillar, the upper part being slotted and jointed at about the middle of the link by a pin, while its lower end is fixed to the pillar on which the pillar top rests. To fold the hood, the cant rails are raised and folded back, the link hinges causing the rear end of the cant rail to leave the face of the pillar, and to turn into a pane parallel thereto, while the lower link hinge causes the pillar to fold down simultaneously. When the hood is fully collapsed, all the parts should be one upon the other, with the usual clearance. To open out the hood the cant rails are raised from their position, assisted by the action of the springs, when the link hinges cause the parts to assume automatically the position shown in the elevation of the drawing (Plate XXIV).

1. The pillar joints.
2. The patent cant rail link hinges.
3. The barrel telescopic springs.
4. Head props.
5. The straight joint ends.
6. The knuckle joints.
7. Elbow prop and stump joint.
8. Front pillar catches.
9. Front pillar hinges.
10. The front joint ends with flap for extension canopy rail.
11. $\frac{5}{8}$ in. knuckle joint.
12. The joint end with flap for front top rail.

CONVERTIBLE FLUSH-SIDED BODY WITH DETACHABLE LIMOUSINE TOP

THE detachable top requires the greatest care and attention to ensure that the lower framework of top exactly fits and coincides with the framework of body on which it rests, the trimming being kept back about 1 in. so that a ledge is formed. Again, the pillar of doors with its rebates must watch the body door, so that glasses may drop freely when top is on, a capping piece fitting on the recess, or if not to drop it may be hinged to top to fold downwards in frame when not required. The front can be made in the folding wind screen pattern or with frames to slide on bottom rail of top, the sides as a rule are fixed—not necessarily so, they can be made to fold in two, hinged in the centre, thus ventilating the top. The whole of the body is fitted with sheet metal steel panel, gauge 20 for bottom where beaten, and 22 for flat and top panels. Apart from the framing and panelling of body, the fit and ease of the detachable top is of paramount importance, and has been the cause of bringing convertible cars into much disfavour. Without going into details of the many and varied methods of fixing the top, I will give for simplicity and ease the following way of securing it rigidly with the set-screw and boss ; if neatly made outside with the front and door inside it proves a satisfactory job. The bottom framing of top may be rebated if preferred, or quite flat with a $\frac{3}{4}$ in. or $\frac{7}{8}$ in. brass or aluminium door plating fixing all round ; this makes a neat and water-tight finish as in Plate XXVII. The top is generally removed by the aid of a block and pulley, and the position of the forged eyes must be found after the top is finally completed, painted and trimmed with glasses and everything. See that the top is balanced, hangs level when pulled up off the body, so that it may be easily dropped on and taken off by one person. The leverage of front and screen has a tendency to tilt the top off, therefore the exact balancing point must be found. The forged eyes are at each corner.

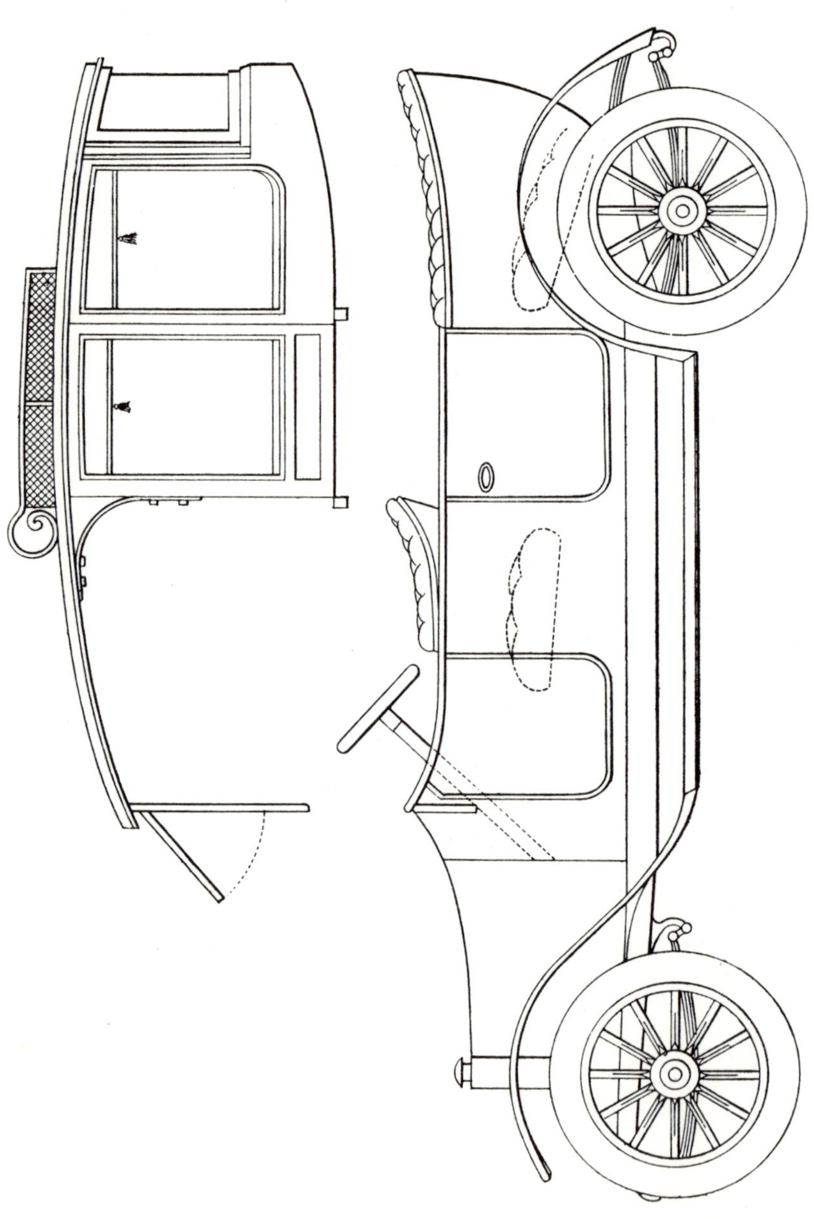

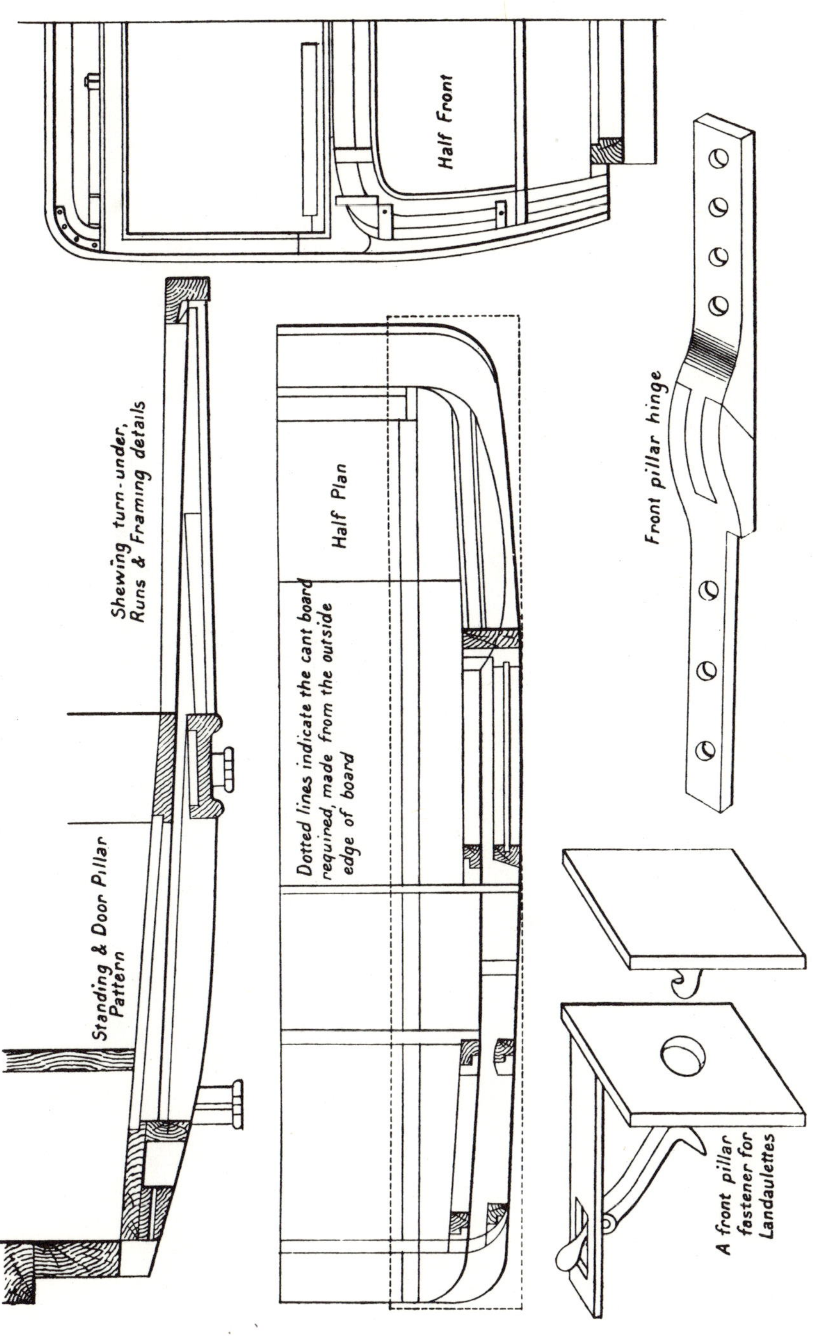
Half Front
Front pillar hinge
Shewing turn-under, Runs & Framing details
Half Plan
Dotted lines indicate the cant board required, made from the outside edge of board
Standing & Door Pillar Pattern
A front pillar fastener for Landaulettes

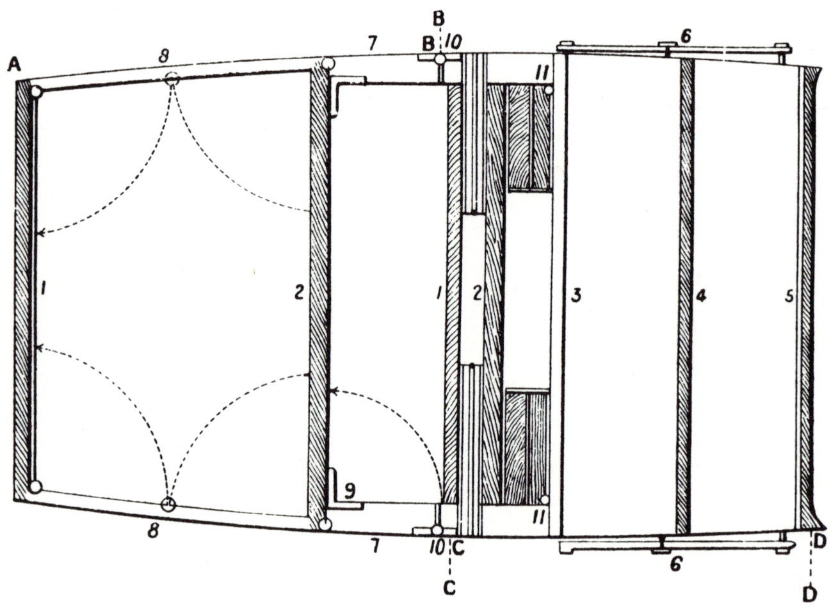

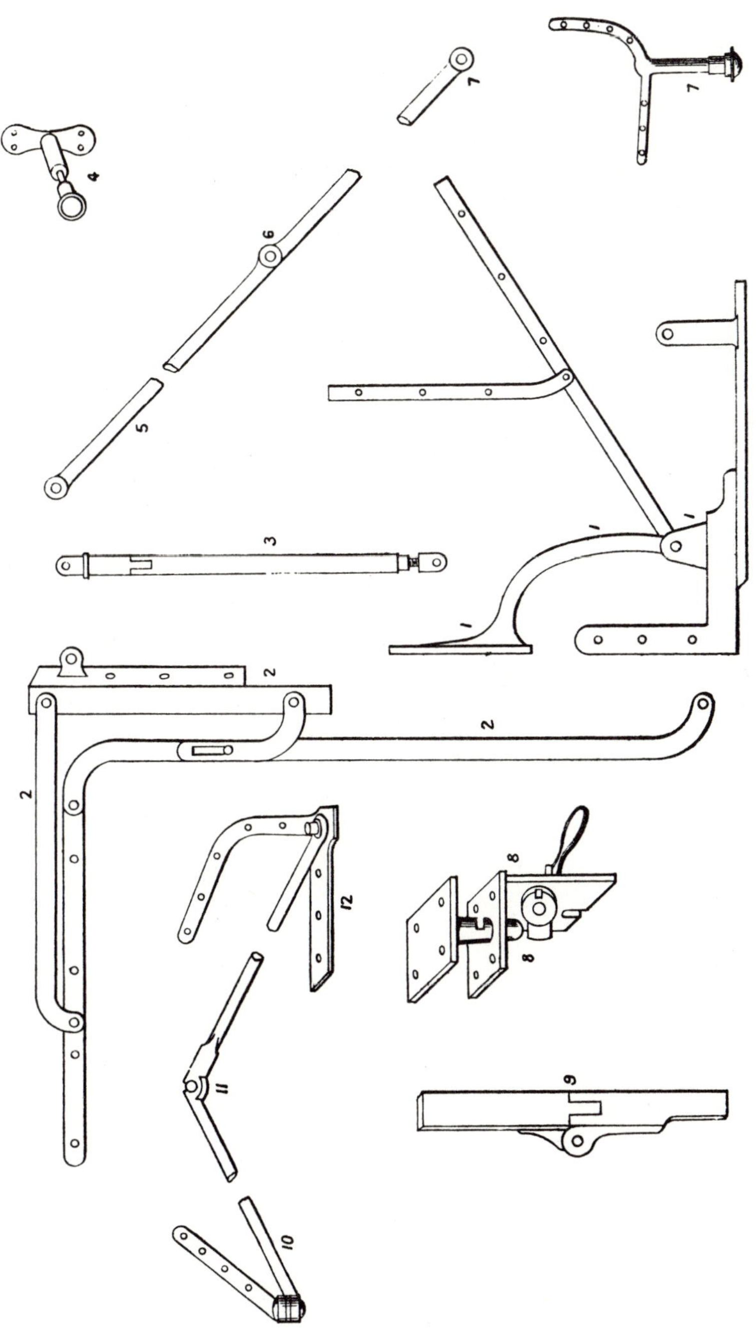

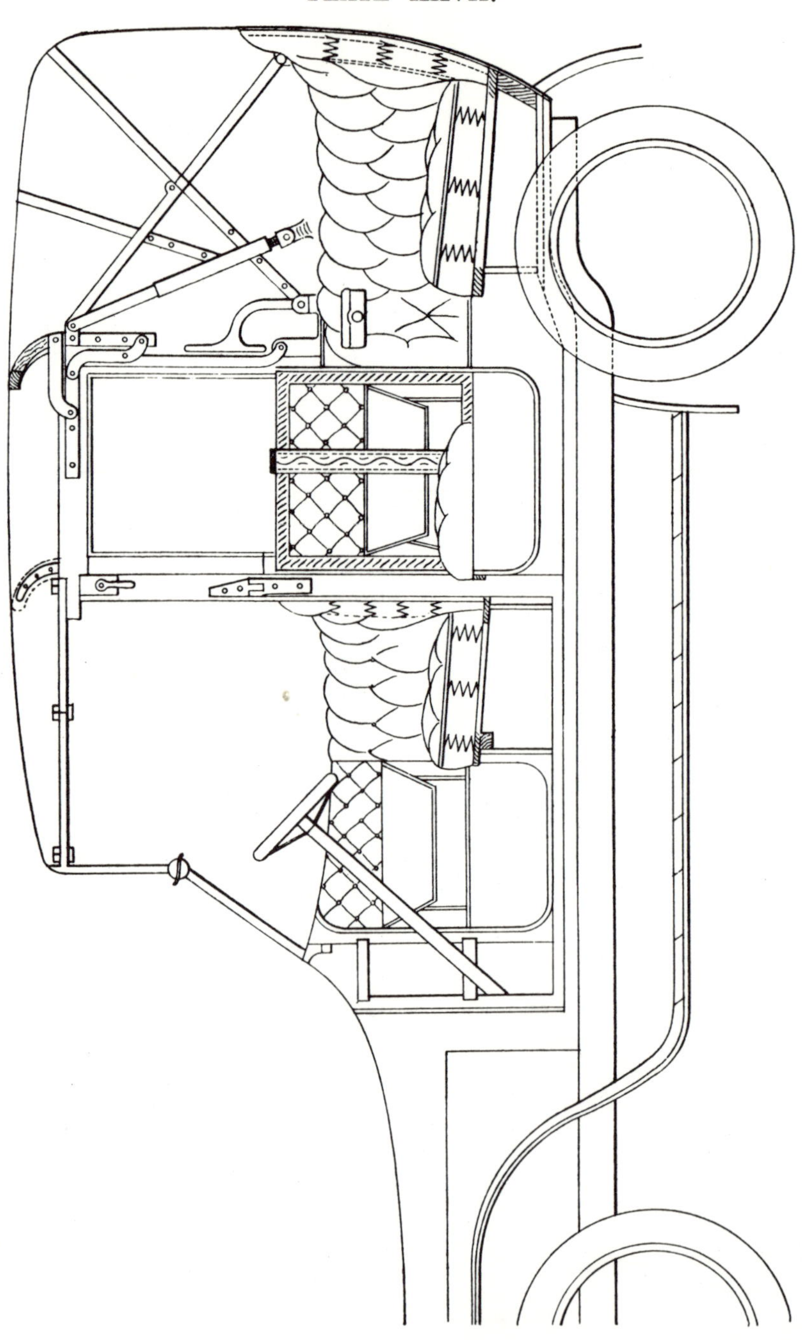

CAPE CART HOODS

(See Plates XLVII and XLVIII)

Numberless varieties of Cape cart hoods are in use, fulfilling the special requirements of owners, but really all can be considered either as the single or double hoods with front extension slats, or the double extension hood entirely operated from the hind part, which latter may be fitted with three, four, or five and, in specially long bodies, with even auxiliary sticks.

The subject of this chapter is not the best or most suitable style, but the method of putting up any or all hoods in a workmanlike fashion. After taking the measurements for the hood, as explained further on, the sticks or slats are ordered from the wood benders. They are sold at per foot (price per set). No more length than is absolutely necessary is ordered, the front and back stick being a trifle under the uniform thickness generally supplied by the trade.

Previous to putting up the hood comes the fixing of the iron work, which should always have stout flaps carried over inside the body (see Plate XLVIII), the hood having possibly to clear the roll over top. In some bodies the slat irons to carry sticks may be bent outwards, thus avoiding the use of a long projecting stay.

After fixing the ironwork, see that it lines crossways and upwards, that the slat irons are true, free from twist and fall nicely into their place. The body flaps and stays, where possible, should be bolted rather than screwed.

Assuming the ironwork is fitted, and that we have a, say, four-stick hood for a side entrance (a general pattern), the front when down is taken by a slotted eye and butterfly nut. We proceed by putting up our centre stick, or the two middle sticks; that will give us the total height, say 3 ft. 4 in. from top of cushion. Before separating the sticks from wood benders, it is as well to mark the centre and square it all over the sticks and set a distance each side some 14 in. or 15 in., and square that over as a test line in measuring the parallelism of sticks to the body.

In the four-seater we have put up our rear seat stick, which is probably square, and the one behind the driver, so to have about 1 in. sail back, and with a light screw fixed temporarily; we now fix the back stick, giving the necessary round or drop for the curvature from front to back, also a sail over the back of 2 in. or 2½ in.; after which we fix each stick—to line

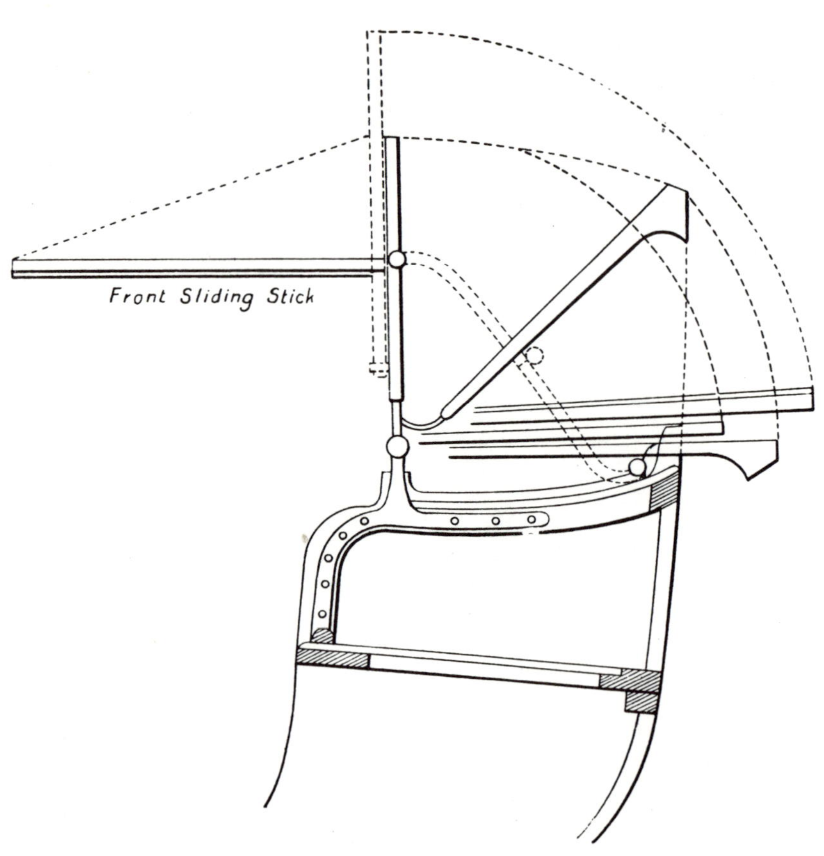
Front Sliding Stick

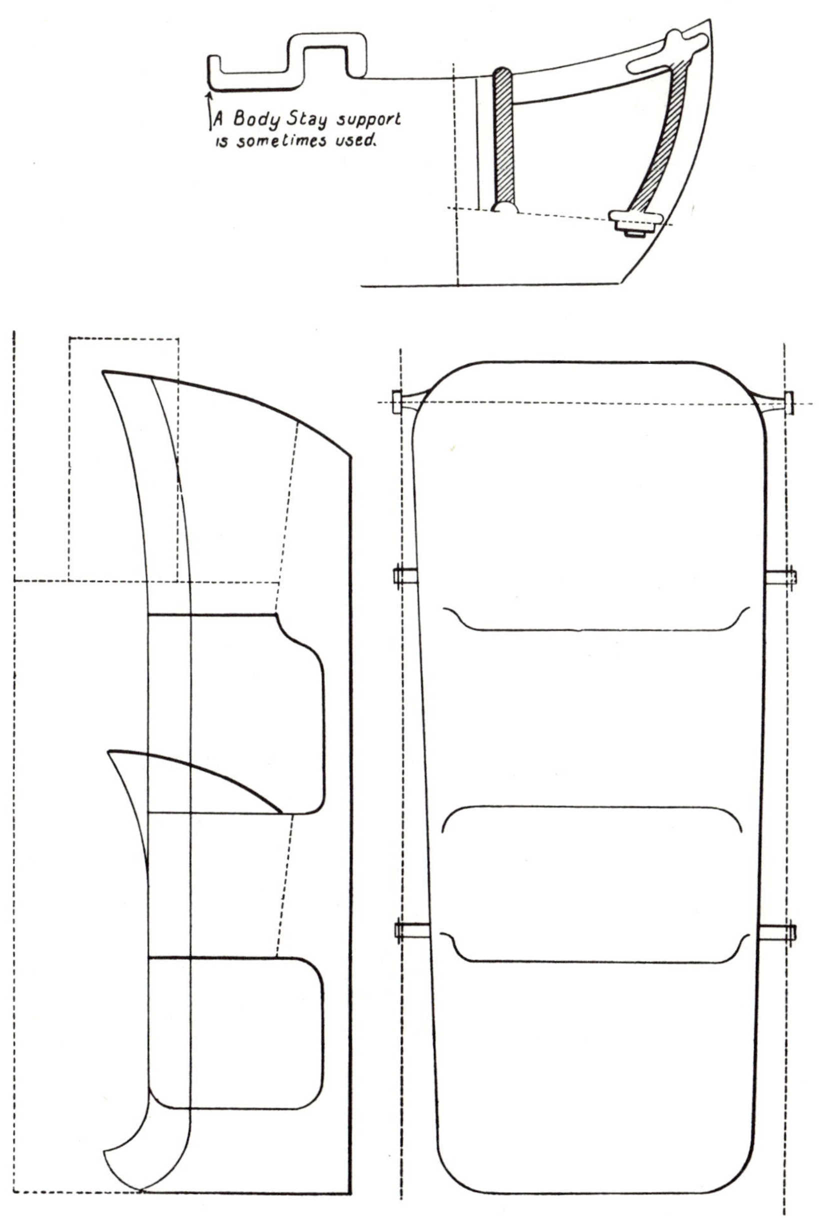
A Body Stay support
is sometimes used.

it, dropping it down and measuring from the points marked from some
part of the body, also cross lining it and well righting the same, as to
improve the appearance one may have to go up a screw hole, or
another down.   All being temporarily fixed and held in place by webbing, the
hood is lowered altogether, and tested for the right clearance between each
stick, not less than $\frac{1}{4}$ in. being given, or more if desired for a special fitting.
Everything being satisfactory, all holes are marked in slat iron, the end of
sticks regularly marked off for length, the sticks are taken off, the ends
rounded and the sticks cleaned up with all sharp edges rounded, then they
are ready for polishing or staining, after which they are varnished, and finally
fixed to the fittings, which may be painted, wrought iron being filed or
all over brass or nickel-plated, as the case may be. If outside stretcher
joints are not used, straps secure the front hood when up. If all is right
the hood is now ready for webbing corners and passing on to trimmer.

The measurements for a hood should embrace the following :—

Head room required.

Depth of body sides at both seats.

Width across body at bracket fixing over the collars, with allowance for
the clearance, giving width inside of sticks.

Length over all.

Shape of corners so as to coincide with body framing.

Contraction, if any, rarely given.

Method of fixing finger plates inside or out of sticks.

Dimensions of each stick in width and thickness.

Length of stick required.

Width across back and front seats and across centre of head rest.

With the above remarks in your mind you can easily follow the dotted
lines in Plates XLVII and XLVIII.

Victoria Leather Hoods, with or without Outside Head Joints.—The
method of putting up hood, fixing slat irons and getting the fittings follow
in this type of body as in the Cape cart hoods ; the accompanying sketch
shows the methods of testing, also the variety of outside stretcher joints
that may be used.   When there are no spring lifting agents the head must be
bound firmly into its position, and the sticks in so doing may be moved a
little either way to suit the eye of the line of curve and the angle of the front
and back sticks, all the sticks being up and set with the requisite pitch and
the sail of the back as seen in the two seater, in which the back stick is made
with a square corner.

The lining of the sticks is shown in Plate XLVIII with the method of
squaring off to form the corners and fixed points.   The front is lined with
the dash transversely as a square point.   The back slats are also lined with
the body framing. While keeping to the measurements, hoods should
be fixed up so as to satisfy the eye, especially in a curvilinear body.   The
hood is now ready for the smith to take the length of the joints.   The

elbow props and top prop nuts should be fixed some 6 or 8 in. down, keeping them, as a rule, as high as possible. These points being fixed, we proceed to take the length of the joint by straining a wax line (having a loop at each end) round the cylindrical ends of the props. The head is then opened or struck to the position it is intended to occupy, making due allowance for the cloth and leather, or twill, or other fabric used in covering. The wax line is then doubled to an angle, lining with the slats, keeping the upper part of joint parallel with the face of front stick, a marking awl holding the corner taut ; a piece of string can be tied in the angle. With double joints the practice is followed from each pair of prop nuts. The wax line is now straightened out on a piece of board fitted with pegs the same size as the

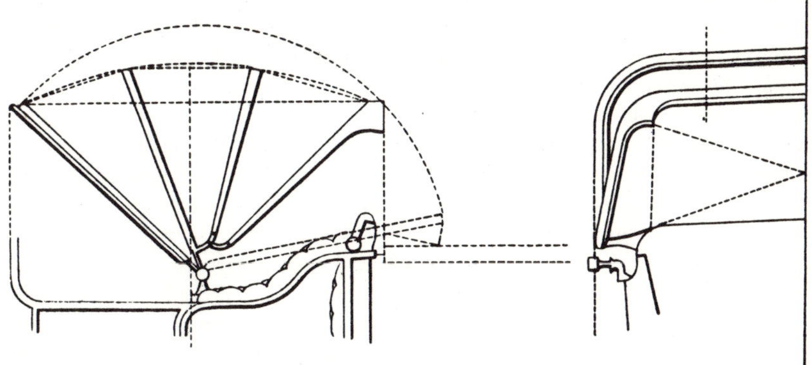

props, and the smith shuts up his joints accordingly, having the joints a good $\frac{3}{8}$ in. or $\frac{1}{4}$ in. longer than the wax line, so as to strain the head tight, and to impart firmness and the necessary set or support to the joint, and so obviate any liability of dropping. This string method is the general way of taking the length of joints as to centres, whatever may be the shapes, though with standard types of bodies iron stretchers with set-holes are frequently used. Straight joints require great accuracy in fitting, so that they line when up and set nicely when down.

Swept shape joints are easy to fit, for the compass may be taken out or put in, as the case may be, with no trouble. All joints should give the " nip " to the head that will set it firm when the covering is on. The size of joints used are $\frac{1}{2}$ in., $\frac{5}{8}$ in. or $\frac{3}{4}$ in. All leather hoods should in front be finished with a valance either of wood, metal or leather, or combination of these materials. A good finish in front is made by fixing a wood valance, and covering the same with the best border leather with a $\frac{3}{8}$ in. metal bead in the centre.

Landaulette and Landau Hoods.—Apart from the details already mentioned, there are one or two important points that it is necessary to emphasize and to make clear for good results and a perfect fitting hood.

The substance of the pillar tops and cant rails are in accord with the lower framing according to depth shown on drawing, being mostly cut from 2 in. to $2\frac{1}{2}$ in. plank; the pillars are rebated $\frac{5}{16}$ in. for frames, if supports are not used, and the four slats mostly used are cut from $1\frac{1}{4}$ in. or $1\frac{1}{2}$ in. ash, worked up $1\frac{1}{8}$ in. or $1\frac{1}{4}$ in.; the hoopsticks are $1\frac{3}{4}$ in. by $1\frac{1}{8}$ in., notched and screwed to the slats from the top with two screws, the whole of the corner being canvased. The pillars in a light landaulette are frequently finished $1\frac{3}{4}$ in., shaped to the top half of hinge pillar, so that all is level inside for the trimming. Most folding hoods are said to be automatic; that is, they depend for their action on the use of spiral springs working either by compression or extension. The main differences in many instances exist in the turning of the cant rail, and the foreshortening of the hood when it folds, so that outside head joints are dispensed with, and that the head may be opened from the inside when the car is running. The connexion of the inside joints with the cant rail renders it then to some extent self-acting. In the mechanism of a good head lift, the springs are enclosed in tubes working telescopically. The application of the spring is varied with most makers, some working up the pillars, some above and some below the elbow, some at an angle and others horizontal, but all having the one desired object with various connexions at the top end of the spring. A great point to study in all spring heads is that the lower axis of the tubes containing the springs must lie in a parallel direction to the pillar when the head is down; this will reduce the power required to lift and also the liability of the head to rise when the car is at work. Cost, weight and simplicity of mechanism, and accuracy in working with the least amount of exertion are the desiderata of these head fittings. In fitting up the heads, be sure that the cutting off of the pillars is in a perfect line with the door rail. The door rail should always be made equivalent to the space occupied by the slats and pillar top, when down, so that the whole is as flat as possible, without the thickness of the folding pillar standing above the hinge joints. Only those hinges should be used that will allow of this, and therefore give a straight line from the door fence rail.

When the hinges are fitted the folding pillars are cut to the length, the cant rail fitted and boxed out for glass frames. Accuracy and the squareness in fitting, as before mentioned, is important, so that when up or down the cant rail is thrown out or folds all in a line. This completed, the thimble catches. Cup, ball or other fittings used to draw them into place may be fixed. In pronounced cabriolet bodies it depends on taste and possible requirements, and also the type of body, as to what amount of droop from the centre to the back and the front and the upward curve of the hoopstick without touching, but in an ordinary landaulette it may be taken as a rule that the centre of the head slats should not curve more than $1\frac{3}{4}$ in. from the centre to the end slat, and should not curve more than $1\frac{1}{2}$ in. to 2 in. on the top.

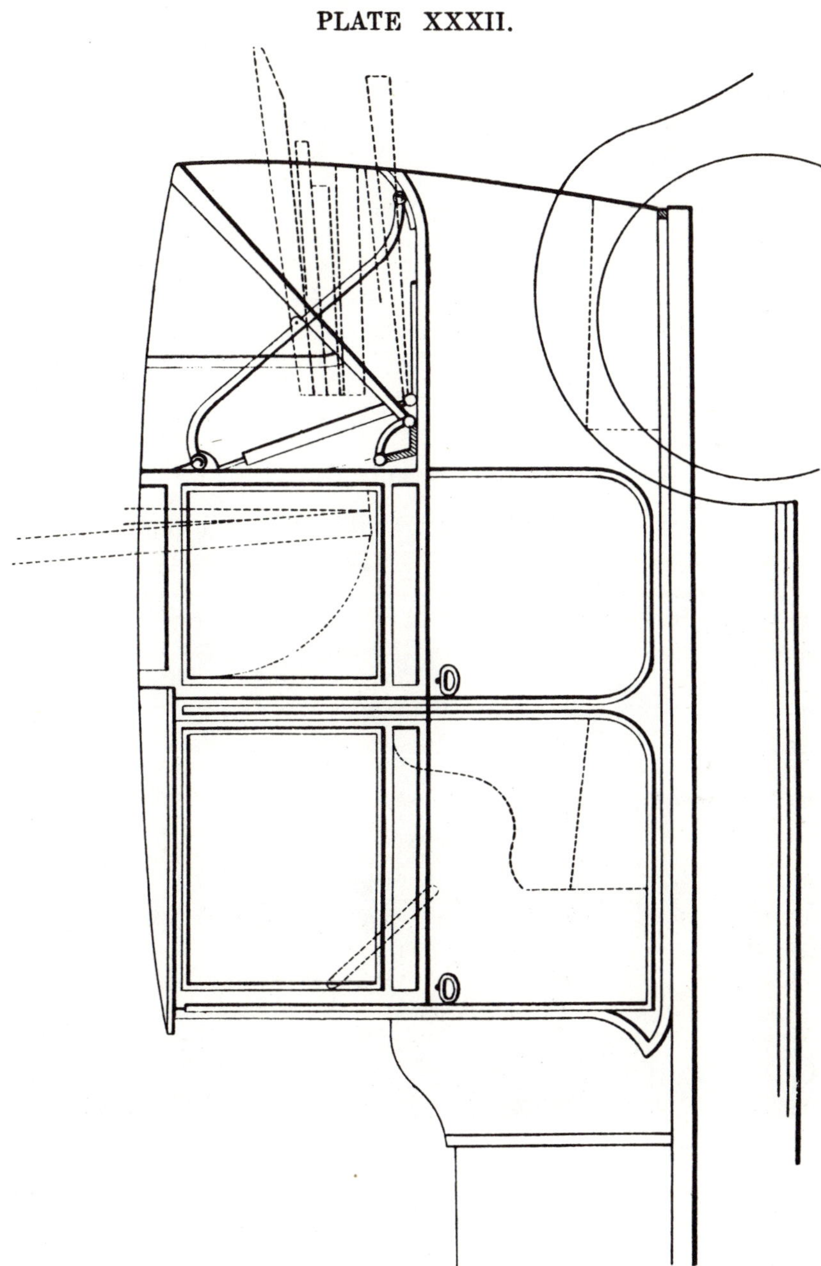

ENCLOSED CABRIOLET

THIS body (Plate XXXII) was designed for a 38 H.P. Daimler, four cylinders, and was built with two doors on the nearside and one on the offside. The front seat is built in one, but trimming pieces are fitted to form bucket seats. The centre pillar folds and drops on back of front seat; the front pillar remains standing, but the top rail is to be made to go back with the head. The top rail is fixed with " Beatson " cabriolet screen fittings which allow the top half of screen to swing. The back portion of cant rail drops downwards, the front portion folding back over it. The centre stick moves on the irons as shown, which are long enough to push it out of the way. The back pillars and hoopsticks are fixed altogether, while the usual glass-frame carriers are to be used. The ordinary cabriolet neck joints can be used instead of those shown.

The advantages of this design are that the moving centre hoopstick takes the leather well out of the way, besides keeping it from " sagging " when the head is closed.

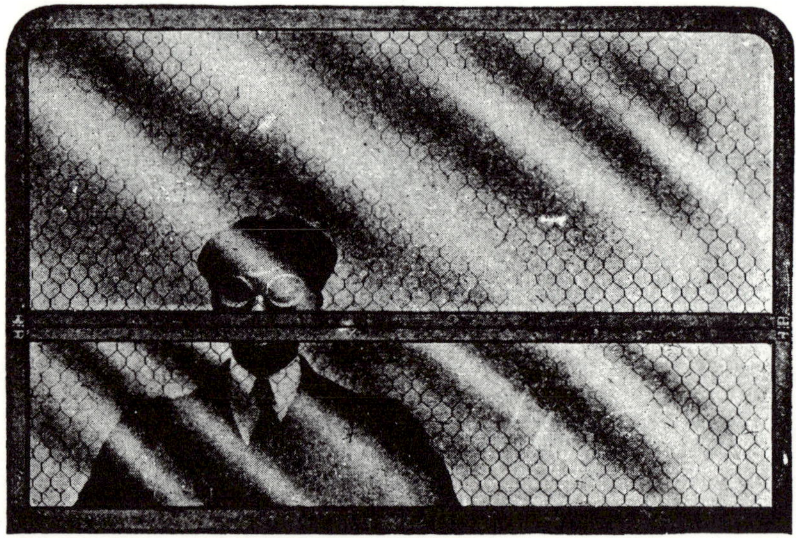

Hires-Turner Glass is glass reinforced with wire. This is polished plate wire glass, which can be bent to any curve desired or furnished flat. It is a guard against accidents, will not shatter if broken, and is perfectly transparent.

GENERAL directions for their arrangement and fitting. It is outside the province of this chapter to advocate any particular type of wind-screen, for all have more or less of the many advantages claimed by the makers. The several patterns now on the market relieve the bodymaker of its selection, which is more often decided by the owner when ordering. Notwithstanding, it is important that the bodymaker should thoroughly understand the proper functions of a screen in order to avoid the faulty application, unsound mechanism and a wrong principle frequently seen on otherwise high-class work. The utility of a screen is, of course, comfort and the complete protection of the occupants, especially on the front seat, from all back draught, wind, dust and rain; and these results must be obtained without in any way obstructing the view of the driver in bad weather.

The screen in its fixing must be firm, rigid, neat in appearance, light in weight, free from rattle, and easily adjusted when the car is running, and frequently special requirements are needed, if the car is to be exported. Wind-screens, though of many patterns, may really be classified under the following headings :—

The upright plain single screen, rigidly fixed to the dasher or behind front seat ;

The single-folding upright, or fixed at an angle and made to fold or revolve in any direction ;

The double-folding or triple-folding screens, with deflecting glass panel that can be adjusted at any suitable angle ;

Special types of screens to fit dash with swept panels; and screens are panelled with other materials than glass (as frequently on the Continent), consisting of an iron frame covered with canvas or enamelled leather at its upper or lower part. Screens for cars for hot climate are frequently of wire gauze. Screens are also panelled with polished plate, with wire imbedded, as at No. 6 (Plate XLIX), for safety, as also are screens of the " Vene Triplex," which is a triple substance of glass, celluloid and glass, the object being, of course, in case of an accident there will be no cuts from broken glass.

In fixing the screen and deciding on the dimensions of the folding panels, be careful to arrange for the diversion of air currents, by different adjust-

PLATE XLIX.

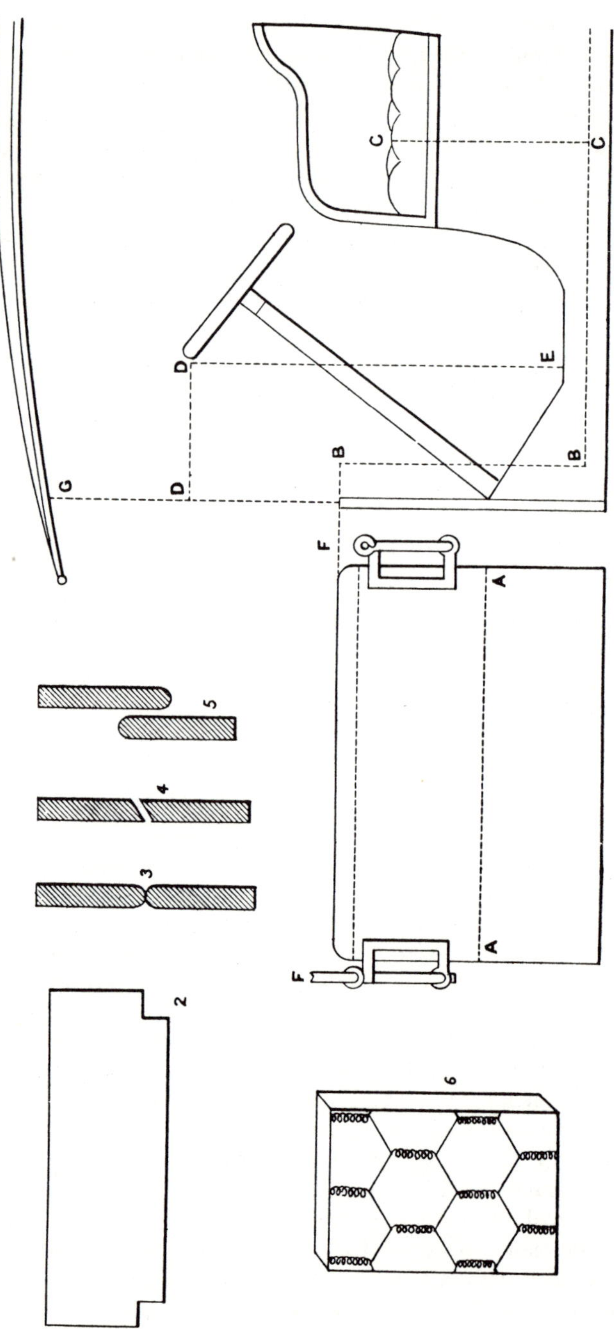

ments, in order that all moisture should disappear quickly, thus giving a clear view through the panes. In a car for India wire gauze should always be fitted and kept low enough to enable the occupant to see the road ; the top edge is kept 18 in. to 20 in. from the driver's face, so that it breaks the wind with no back draught ; but if kept higher, then an open mesh is required for driver to see through. The mesh in common use is 36 to the inch. Measurements, of course, vary for different bodies, but for an ordinary torpedo body, with hollow dash, approximately 4 ft. over all, all reasonable demands should be met by a standard size with a depth of top frame from 12 in. to 13 in., with the folding deflecting frame 6 in. to 8 in. deep.

A limousine body frame varies from 3 ft. 8 in. to 3 ft. 10 in., small single screens 3 ft. 3 in. to 3 ft. 6 in., rarely less than 3 ft. 4 in., or otherwise the many advantages are lost. The sizes of the walnut or mahogany wood frames should be $1\frac{3}{4}$ in. by $\frac{3}{4}$ in., supported by $\frac{3}{4}$ in. half round or $\frac{5}{8}$ in. stanchions, to which they are fitted and sometimes clipped, or working entirely in a metal frame.

When the top frame is made to swing, with a metal frame all round, the rails may be kept $1\frac{1}{8}$ in. wide. The best joint in making the frame is the mortise and tenon, and to ensure the tight fitting of glasses, especially with open end frames, the shoulders should be cut slightly bevel to bring the frame $\frac{1}{4}$ in. in on top, so as to cause a nip. However strong the windshields, stays and brackets may be, and however well fixed, vibration and rattle will set up if the dash be not rigid, and if it is at all on the weak side it should be stayed by a stout bracket, which may be fixed or adjustable, especially when, as frequently happens, the lamp bracket may be in the solid. The complete fittings are now supplied, leaving little or nothing to the body-builder beyond the fixing, though it is the common practice of many bodymakers to make and fit their own screens, making their own ironwork and often all fittings, having them all over brassed, close-plated or nickelled, and thus screens are made at once suitable for the job in hand. In doing this it is as well for the bodymaker to remember to have the fewest number of parts or any complicated mechanism ; to see that the adjusting handle is large, easy to move, and that the ironwork has sufficient strength, so that the screen will stand up against wind pressure, and not eventually set up vibration by parts working loose. As to the various fasteners, silences, channeling and other fitments required by special body work, their construction is simplicity itself and attachment self-explanatory.

Fitting up Bent and other Glasses.—It frequently happens that trouble is found by the bodymaker in putting in bent glasses so that when fixed and at work they will not "fly" or fracture. The causes of fractures in many cases are that the rebating on the framework is not true, that the framework is not rigid and works slightly, that the glasses are unevenly bedded, thus causing unequal pressure on the fillets.

Taking the bent corners in landaulette with **D**-front, I would insist on a plate ¾ in. half round up on the inside of the pillar with a flap along top bent corner. The glasses should be put in from the inside, not out; to keep the water, etc., away. The framework is then fitted round to the glass, so that it lies dead home and there is no movement in any corners and no spaces can be seen from the outside; the fillets are then screwed in, after which the glasses are removed, and the frame painted round the rebates. In final fixing, cover the edges with thin sheet rubber, paint the framework with a coat of gold-size, take two hand-shavings off the fillets, and screw into place. The draw on the screw-holes gives sufficient pressure on the rubber to bed the glass, and when all is hard and dry, clean off the gold-size that squeezed out with a sharp bevelled-edge chisel. This is more effectual than putty or red lead, etc., that only work out cracks, etc., and, what is more, running vibration in the car will not have the least effect on glass bedded in this manner. The frames are jointed with slip, mortise and tenon, but to ensure that glasses which have an open end are tight, the shoulder should be cut slightly bevelled, as already stated.

With patent folding frames, either for front or back, special instructions are usually given as to the fitting. The patent or invention itself usually consists only of the attachment, locking or adjusting arrangement, and an individual can make without fear any type of shape, whether to slope or to fold, using his own idea as to securing the same.

Patent fasteners, metal channeling, metal moulding are frequently used for lightness, strength and rigidity, while telescopic stays with swivel joints are often utilized to prevent cranking the stays. The metalwork, as a rule, is polished all over brass or nickel-plated, " not electric."

In regard to the glass, the best polished plate-glass is used, about $\frac{3}{16}$ in. thick. The sketch, 1 and 2, shows the corners notched to keep the squares fixed in the frames; 3, 4, 5 show the treatment of various edges. The curved polished plate, $\frac{3}{16}$ in. thick, is, as a rule, about 6*d*. per foot more in price than the ordinary glass used. In very cheap work glass known in the trade as 26 oz. or 32 oz. is sometimes used. When glass has to be bent to the frame or patterns, as for **D**-front, it takes six or seven days before the glass is properly annealed after bending.

I have already mentioned about glass, celluloid and glass combined. This kind is on the market and is known as the Triplex Safety Glass. It is quite a new departure and is a great boon for the motor car, where it has many applications for the wind-screens and windows.

The principle upon which this glass is made is strikingly simple. A sheet of specially-selected clear celluloid is placed between two sheets of plate-glass and the three sheets, after a patent treatment, hydraulically pressed together. Owing to the tenacity of the celluloid, when the glass receives a heavy blow it merely bulges out, and " stars."

The following sketches illustrate a test which the makers put this glass

90

to, and shows its usefulness for motors, etc., thus minimizing the danger of cuts in case of accident.

A sheet of the Triplex glass was placed in a frame and mounted vertically. A round iron ball, weighing 2 lb., was suspended on a cord 15 ft. from the ceiling in such a way that, when released, it struck the glass fair in the centre. The force of the blow, it will be fully appreciated, must have been very severe. Nevertheless the Triplex glass was not punctured, it merely bulged out approximately to the shape of the iron ball on the other side of

(1) Ordinary Plate glass.

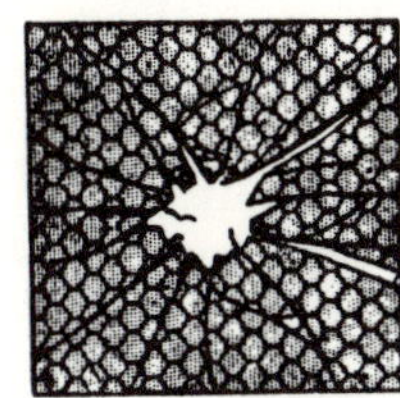

(2) Armoured glass with wire imbedded in it.

(3) Triplex glass.

the glass. Moreover, the glass, although actually fractured or " starred " into a great many pieces, did not splinter or fall away in the least.

The same test applied to ordinary plate-glass completely shattered it, and in a case of a test made with the wire imbedded glass, the suspended weight drove a large hole clean through it, some of the pieces of glass being scattered a considerable distance. The celluloid, being hermetically sealed between the glass sheets, cannot possibly tear, and remains as permanent as the glass itself. It is well known that unprotected celluloid very soon discolours, becomes scratched, and rendered inefficient for the purpose of a screen. Moreover, there is the well-known risk of fire, celluloid being extremely inflammable, whilst the Triplex sheets are perfectly fireproof. An interesting fact, which shows the great tenacity of this glass, is that it can be cut on both sides with a diamond without parting, and to cut it a special process has to be adopted. The sheets can be had in any colour.

One Man Extension Tops

In this number we illustrate and describe five movements of "one man tops," which are advertised and sold by the leading carriage hardware dealers in England.

Fig. 1, with all the bows up, is one of the simplest "one man" extension tops made. A is the main support, one on each side, on which the main bow rests, the rest of the bows being hinged to it.

The rear bows are hinged to B and C, and the two front bows, including the two stays, rest on D, showing that the entire front must be held up by the top material only, except where it locks at the stay joint; but nevertheless it would drop if the top material did not hold it up.

If there is a shorter body all the lengths are reduced in proportion, and the main as well as the back bow are given less inclination. The same is done in the case of a larger body, except in the opposite direction, as all the stays and bows are lengthened and the bows are spread further apart.

The shape of the top can be made to suit. Some prefer a straight line, taking in three bows and then tipping downward front and rear while others taper the tops from the main bow to the front bow in one slight curve and round off on rear bow.

Fig. 2. With bows up, drawn in dotted lines; bows folded, drawn in heavy lines. Note the rear ends of bows drawn in heavy lines, on which the lengths form a straight line; also note the stays drawn in dotted lines, which are all on the inside of the bows.

Making the calculations for a certain length of car the draftsman must first decide the entire length from front edge to rear edge of bows, as our illustrations may be either too long or too short. After the length is obtained the bows, stays and joints are divided on side elevation, at the same time must be folded to obtain the position of the joints; also that the bows when folded have all one length.

All joints must be carried over from the dotted lines with top up, to the heavy lines with top down, as they all must meet exactly, otherwise there will be strain and the joints will bind.

Fig. 3. The heavy lines in this figure indicate the position of top when up on which the main and rear bows rest on the props A, one on each side. The short and long rear bows are hinged, to be of the same length as shown by dotted circular lines B C. On this top are two stays hinged to the main bow D E, and as there is a lock joint at F the front part is held up by joints D E and lock joint F.

When folded, the front bow G is lifted upward, moving bow H with it, while joint F opens, moving toward I, as shown by dotted line, also joint J moves toward K, as shown by circular dotted line. Stay D L moves with bow H and joint J, therefore must be jointed at the center of stay at M. By the movement of G and H, joint M opens and closes automatically same as joint F.

After the top has been drawn to one inch scale or larger and all joints correctly obtained, draw it full size; take strips of wood ¼ x 1 inch; for centers use wire nails, and when all the strips representing the bows and stays are in position as shown on Fig. 3, move the top backward and see how it folds.

If the centers are not in the right position there will be strain, and the top will not fold. The draftsman generally knows where the strain is and removes the wire nail and compares the position of the two holes, and the corrections can then easily be made.

Fig. 4 shows the top up (in dotted lines) and folded (in heavy lines) and includes the circular lines to indicate the movement of the entire top as all the joints must meet from the standing to the folding position. If the top lengths on rear end (shown in the folding position) do not meet they must be shortened or lengthened and the centers changed to equalize all the centers and lengths. This can be done by tracing the movements of upper ends of bows.

Fig. 5 illustrates a top with two supports only, but the movement is different from the others. On Figs. 1, 2, 3 and 4 the entire front part of top is secured to the main bow, but on Figs. 5 and 6 the upper joint is on main bow, while the lower end of the second bow from the front is connected with a rod to the vertical bow.

When the rear end of this stay A moves toward the main bow and upward, the front end B moves downward, pulling at A instead of the main bow. The advantage of this construction is that it eliminates one stay on each side, including the knuckle joint, which, from a constructional view point and in closing and opening the top, is far superior.

When the front part of the top is lifted by the chauffeur the rod C D, which has a stationary joint on C, moves downward on D and B, and at the same time pulls the back part of top from joint A toward the main bows. In other words the upper movement of the front bow helps to draw up the rear part of the top.

All bows which have two or three connections must be well made and all joints well fitted. Rivets should be avoided and ,replaced with machine bolts, but the thread should be always without nuts at the joint and the thread should not extend into the part around which the bow or stay moves.

94

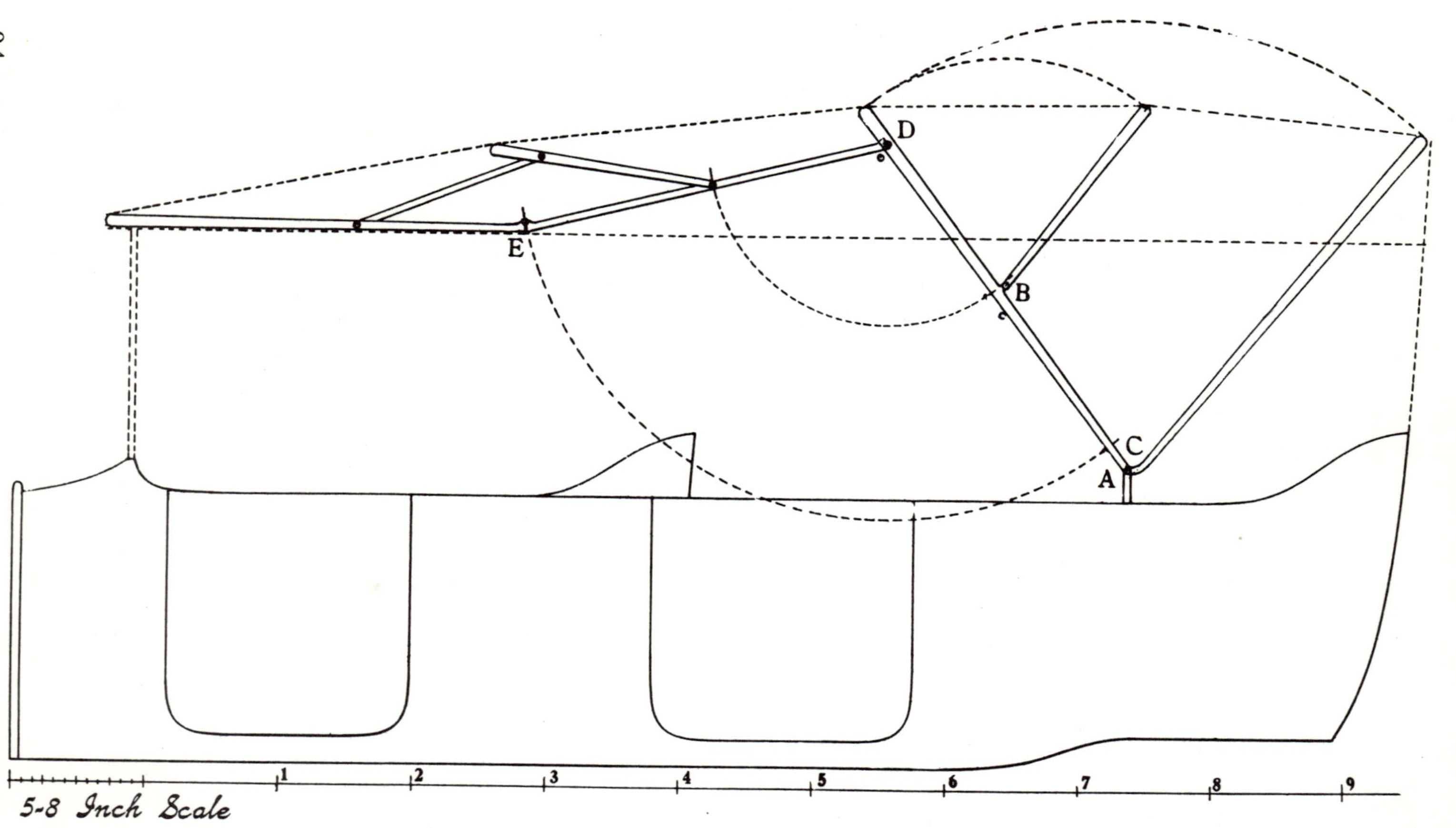

Fig. 1.—The strain on these two tops is entirely on the top cover.   Shown with bows and stays in position.

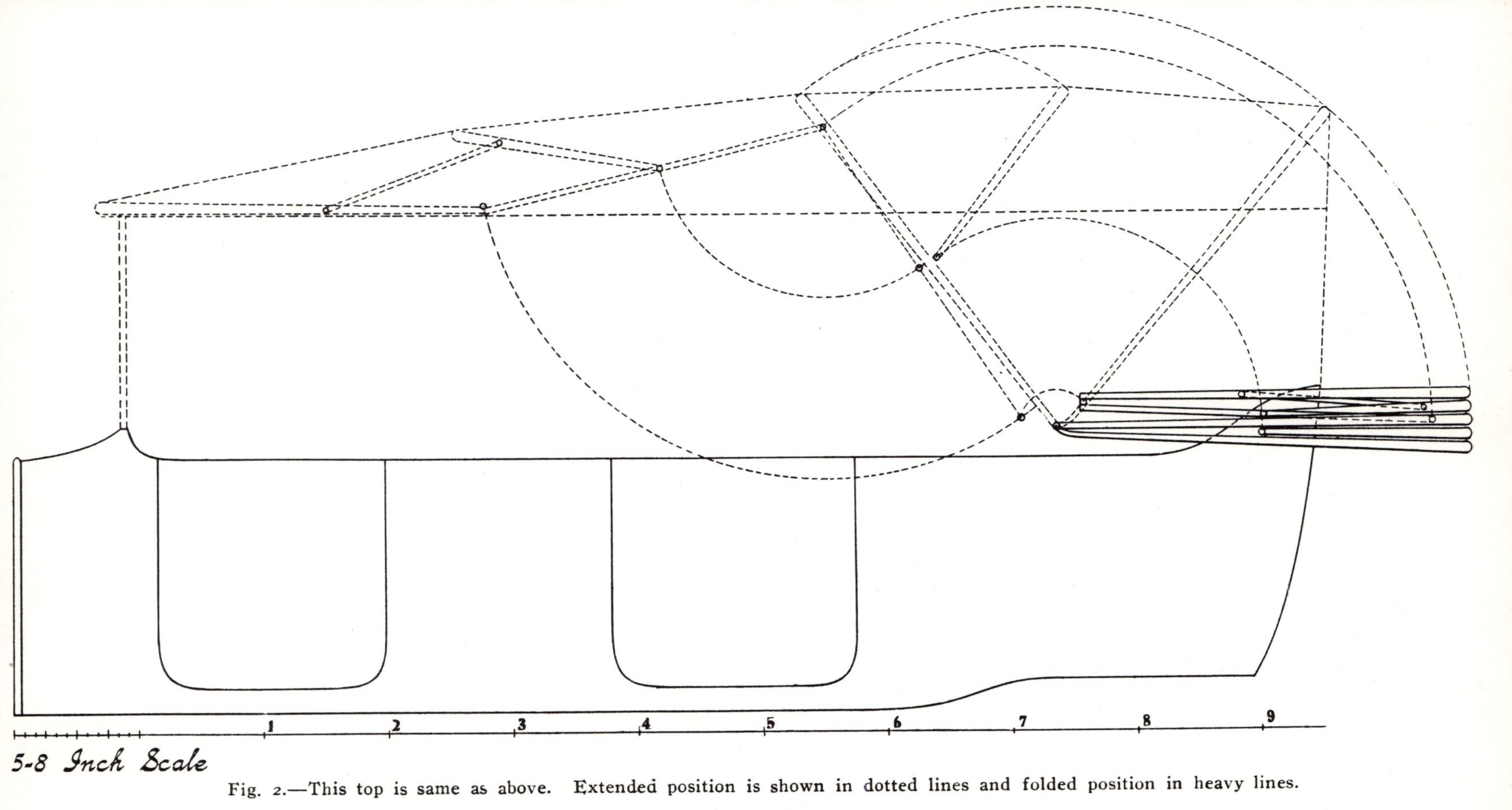

Fig. 2.—This top is same as above. Extended position is shown in dotted lines and folded position in heavy lines.

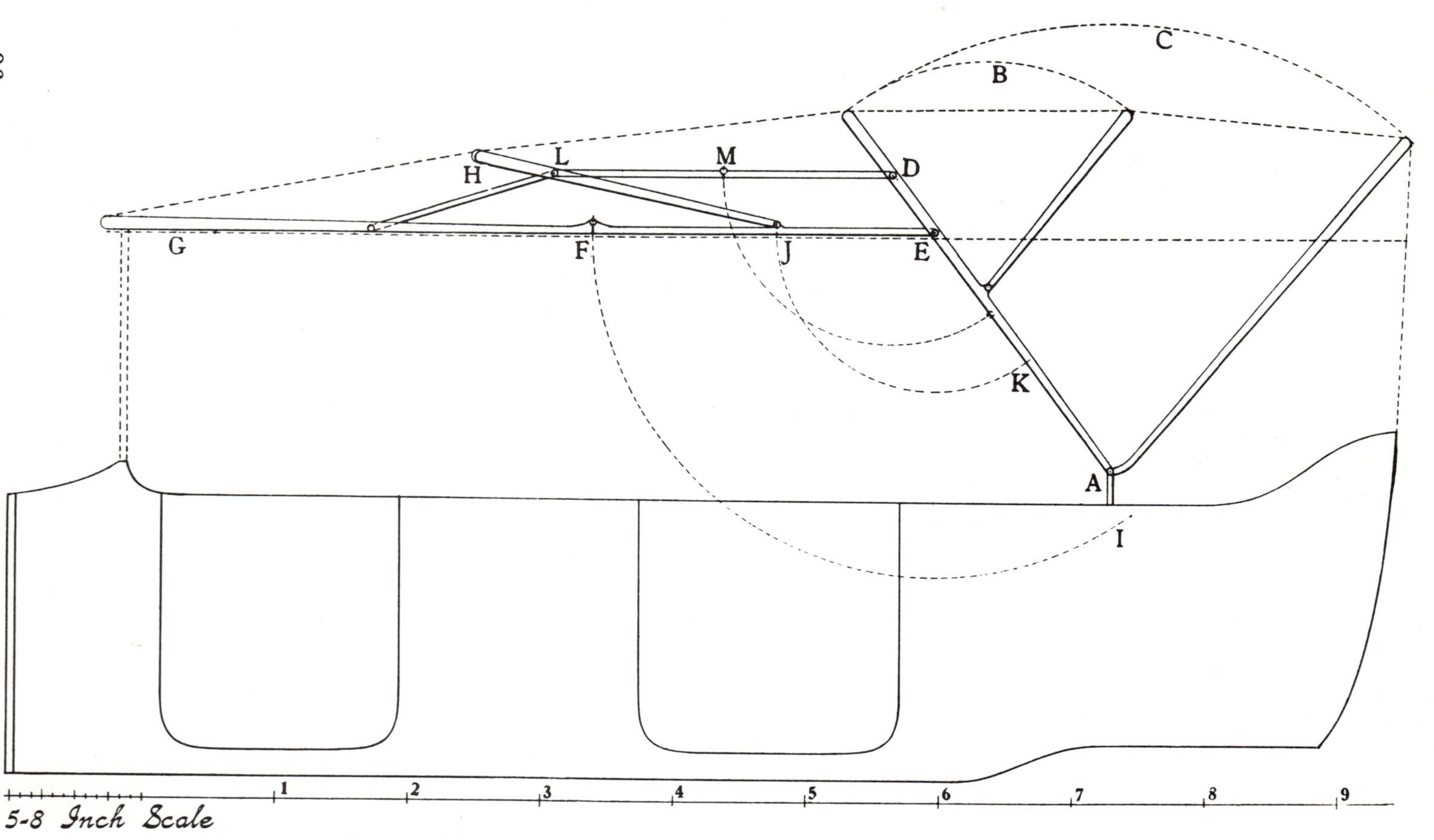

Fig. 3.—These two tops have two stays to support the front part of top.

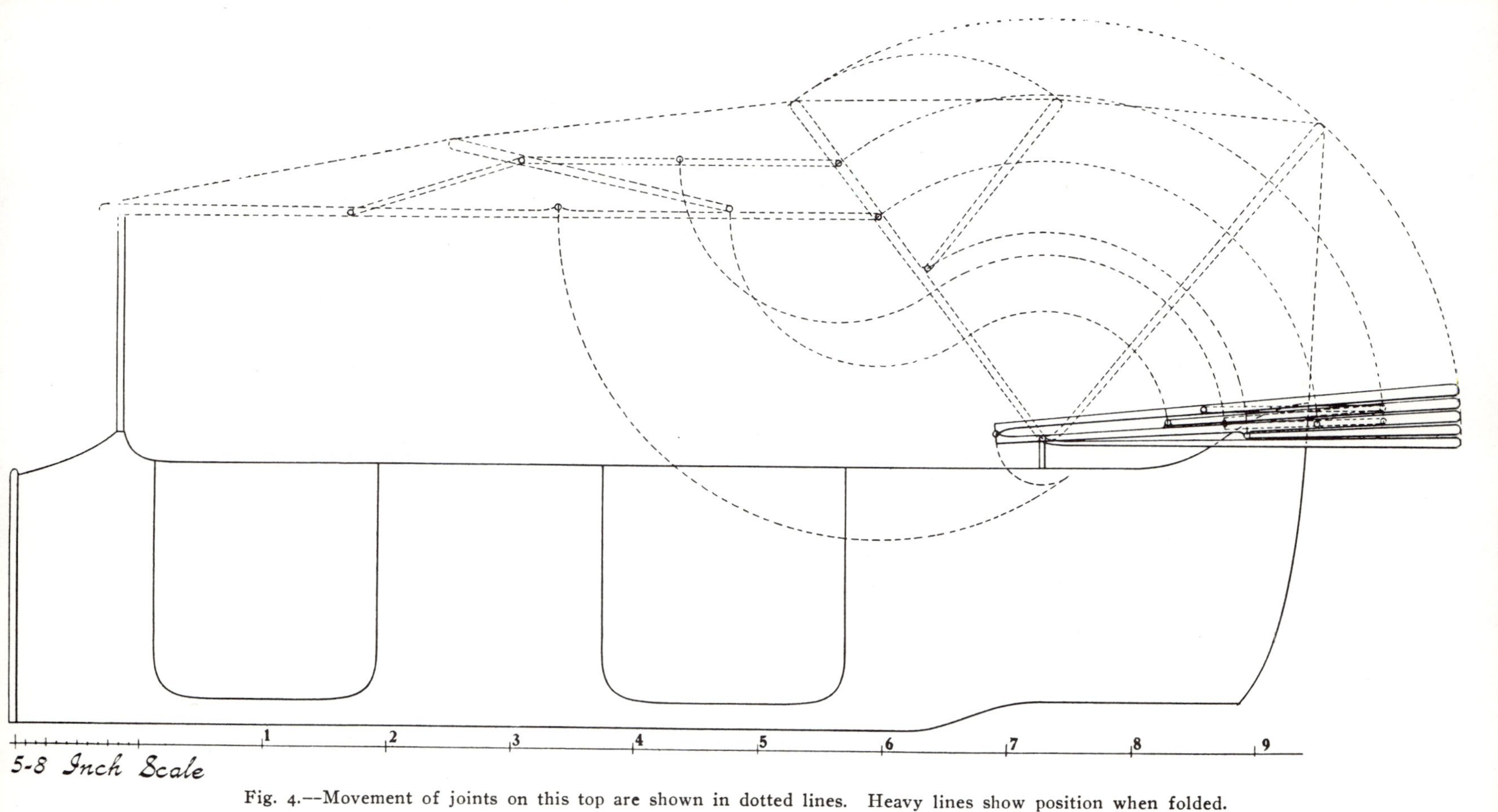

Fig. 4.—Movement of joints on this top are shown in dotted lines. Heavy lines show position when folded.

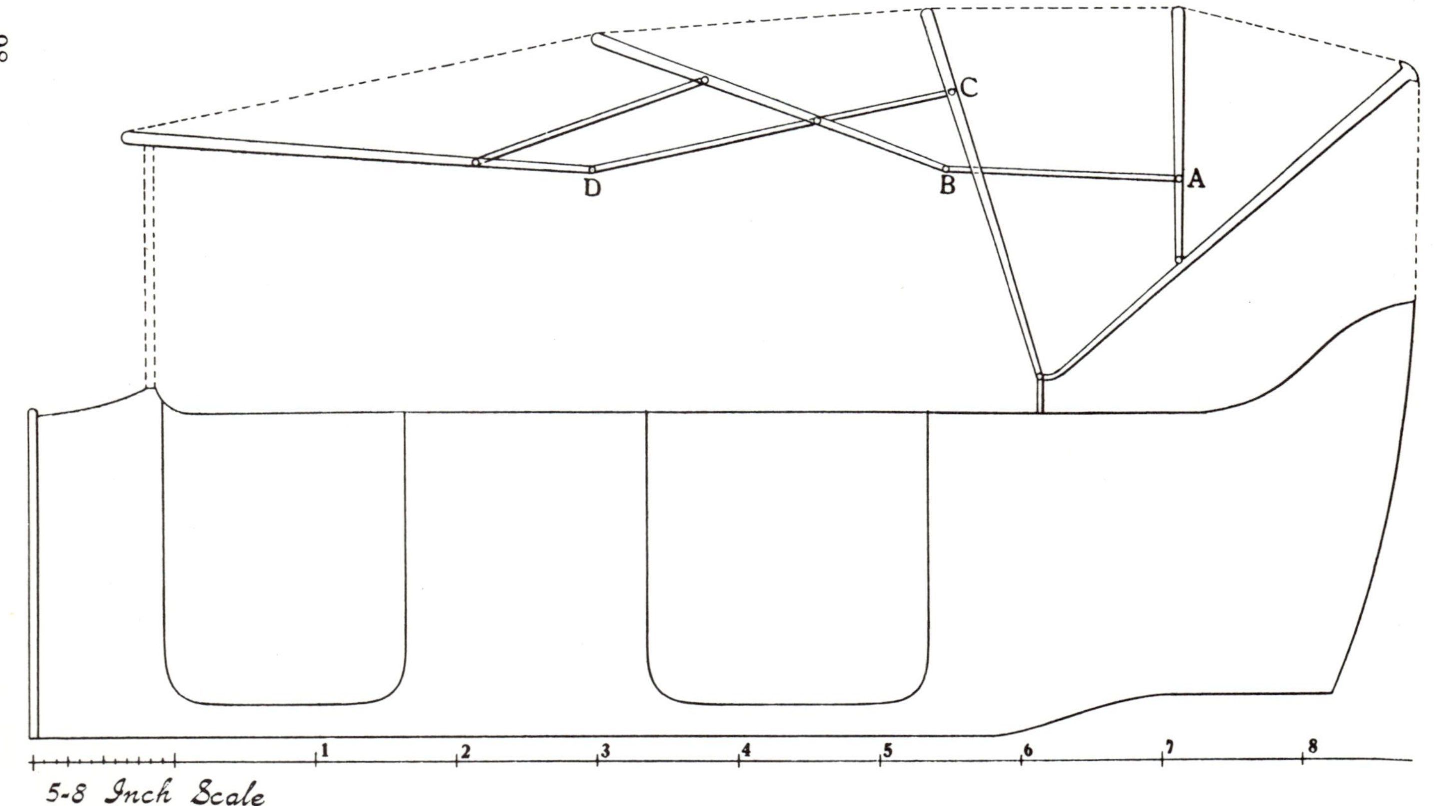

Fig. 5.—Note the joints on this top; when folded all the bows move simultaneously.

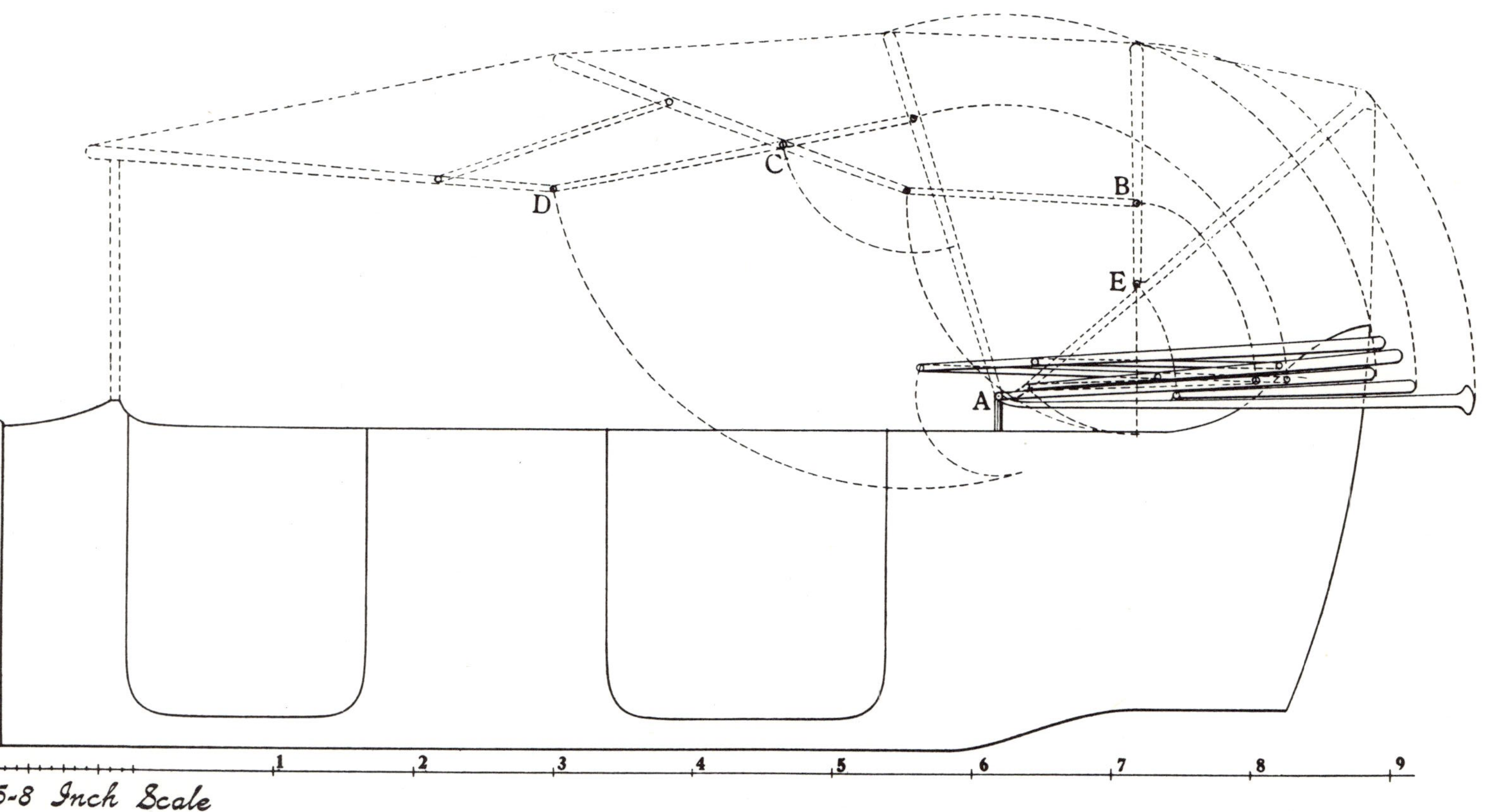

Fig. 6.—Note the top up in dotted lines, bow movement and top down are shown in heavy lines.

Fig. 6 indicates the movement of each bow, stay and joint. Set dividers on joints A, B, C, D, E and follow the circular dotted lines from the standing to the folding position.

On this top the bows are all of unequal length, but the front and second bows can be made shorter. With this system this cannot be easily done with the fourth and fifth bow, but at least the first, second and third bows should be of equal length, which easily can be done by equalizing the spaces.

Figs. 7 and 8 indicate another mode of construction. On this top are two rods, both connected to the main bow and second bow, which makes a strong and simple construction.

All these tops have two supports only, but the correct position on the body must be secured with the top covering, as the weight of the front part of top pulls on the back stays; the front of top pulls on both front and back part.

Because the tops have no top joints the whole pull must be regulated to straighten the top out from the front, but at the same time keep it level with the body line.

If the top covering is too short it will lift the front bow and open the joint on A. Also if the top bows have a full curve the joint B must be lowered to move into the straight line of the bow.

On almost all the systems of "one man tops" there is a stay from C to D, Fig. 7, which holds the second bow well up in the correct position. On Fig. 3, in our May number, this second bow cannot be connected with the rod except by a stop resting against it when the top is up. This stop is on rod E D, below the bow G H. When this rod moves downward it moves away from the stop, but when up, the bow rests on the stop and moves the bow in the correct position. This important part was not explained in our May number.

Fig. 8 illustrates the top in three different positions. The long dotted lines show the top in the correct position when up. The short dotted lines show the front part of the top in a moving position and the heavy outlines show the entire top folded. This will give a thorough inside view of the movement of the entire top.

On this top, when folded, the first three bows drop even on rear end while on the other two the length is evenly divided between them.

In Figs. 9 and 10 we illustrate a touring car or sight-seeing car top which can be made of any desired length and designed in sections, each section for one seat. If the car is desired longer another section is put on. All bows lay flat when folded and all are level at rear end.

The system of folding the top is as simple as in any of the smaller tops. The chauffeur and conductor take hold of the two front standards, which rest in sockets on top edge of body and are hinged to the horizontal bow, and carry and fold the top to the second standard.

Again they take hold of the second standards, in connection with the two first ones, and carry the entire top up to the main bow and tip the six bows flat on the body. All the joints are so arranged that they not only close up, but all bows are even on rear end.

Fig 10 will give a more comprehensive view of the top by showing the movements of the joints in long dotted lines, the movement of the rear bow and connections in short dotted lines, and the movement of the entire six bows in heavy outlines. The movement of the short dotted lines is in itself important when a short back bow is needed, as the bow can not only be shortened but the joints can also be arranged to make all the bows level in the rear.

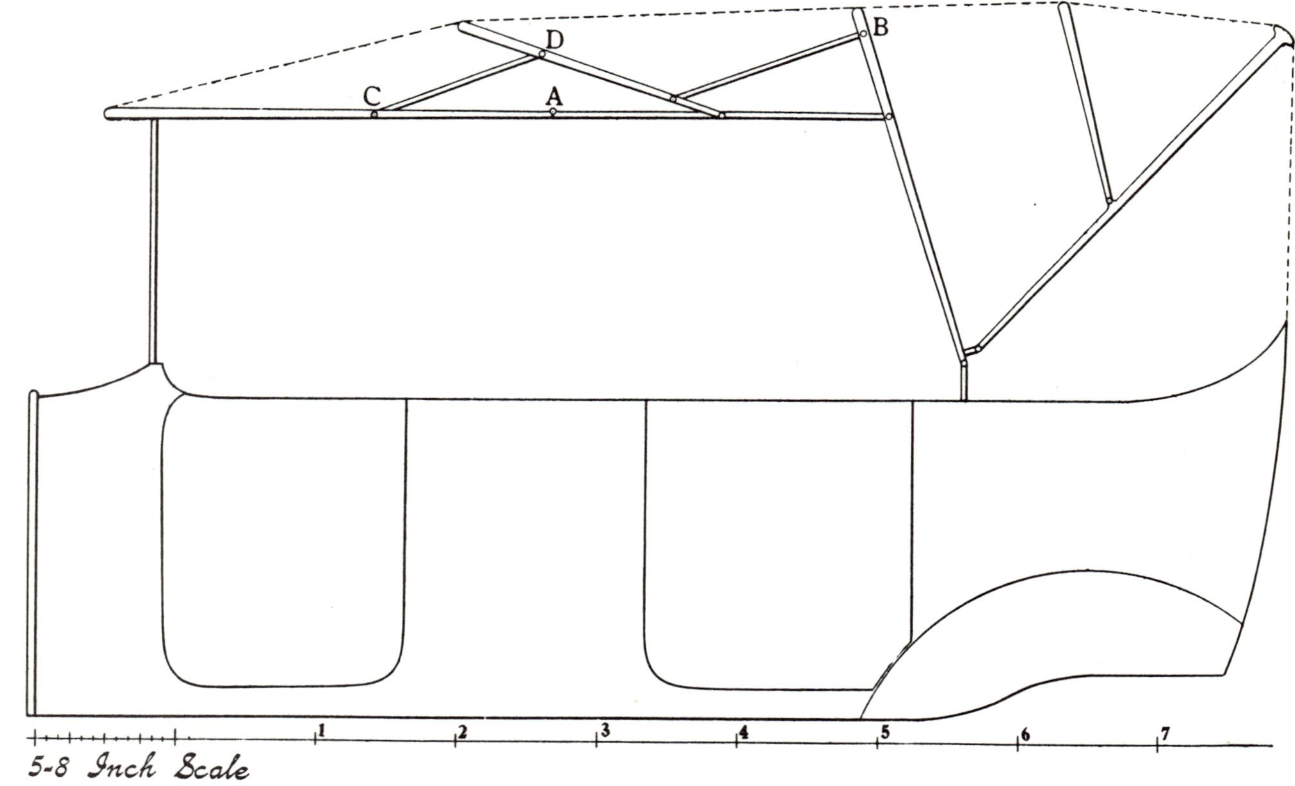

Fig. 7.—Top up in heavy lines.   Two supports on main bow.

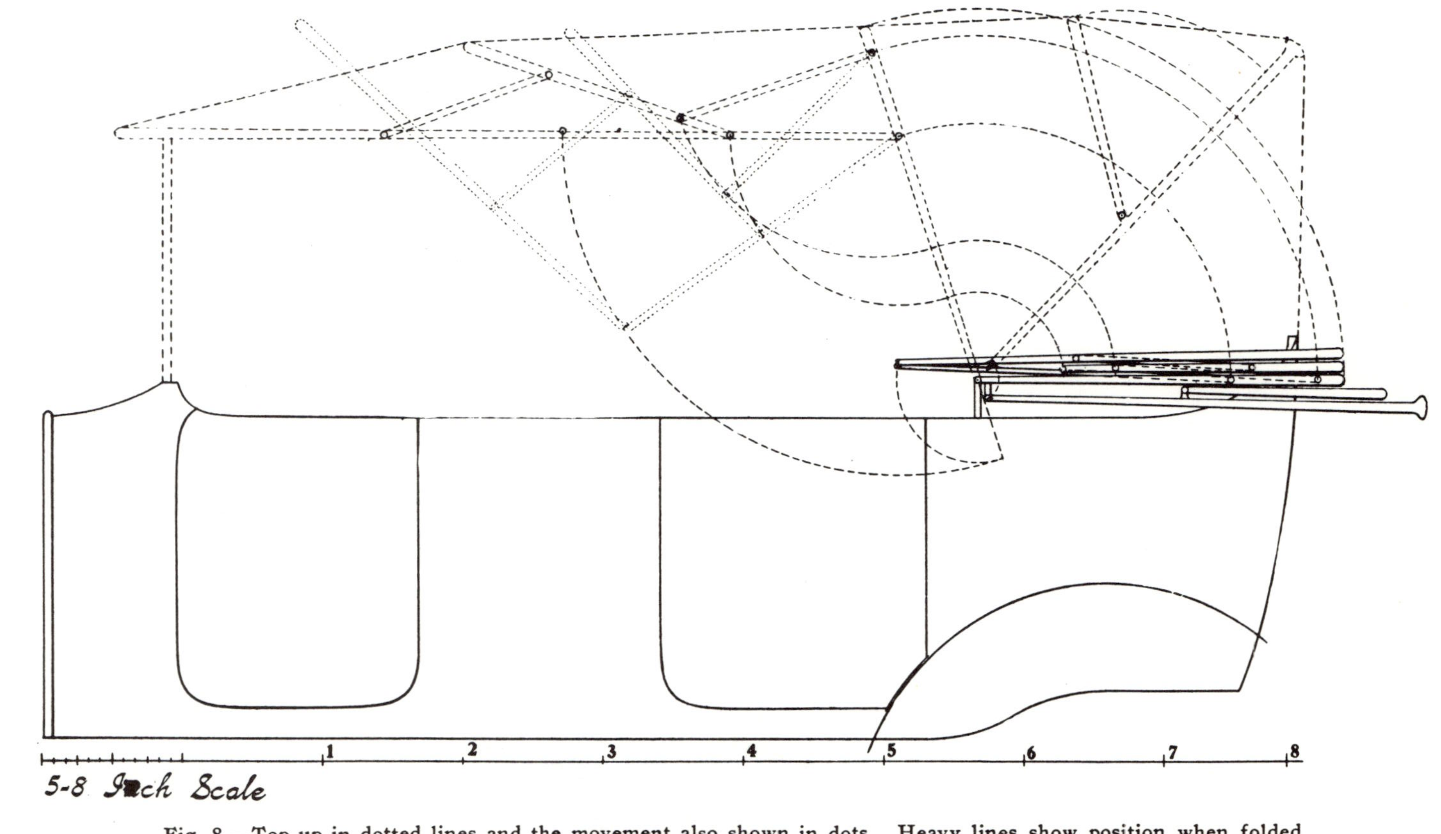

Fig. 8.—Top up in dotted lines and the movement also shown in dots.   Heavy lines show position when folded.

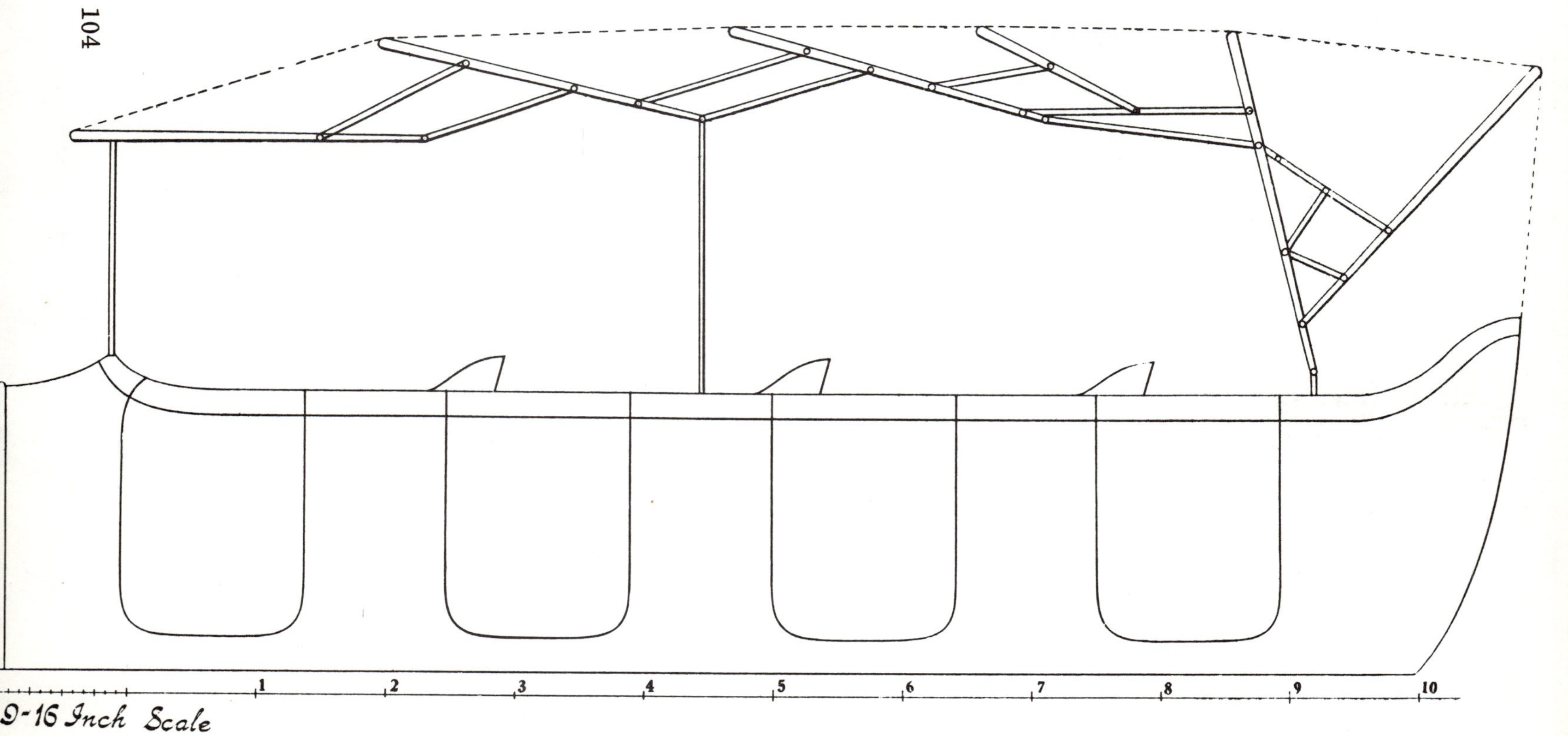

Fig. 9.—Touring car top with six supports. This top can be made any desired length.

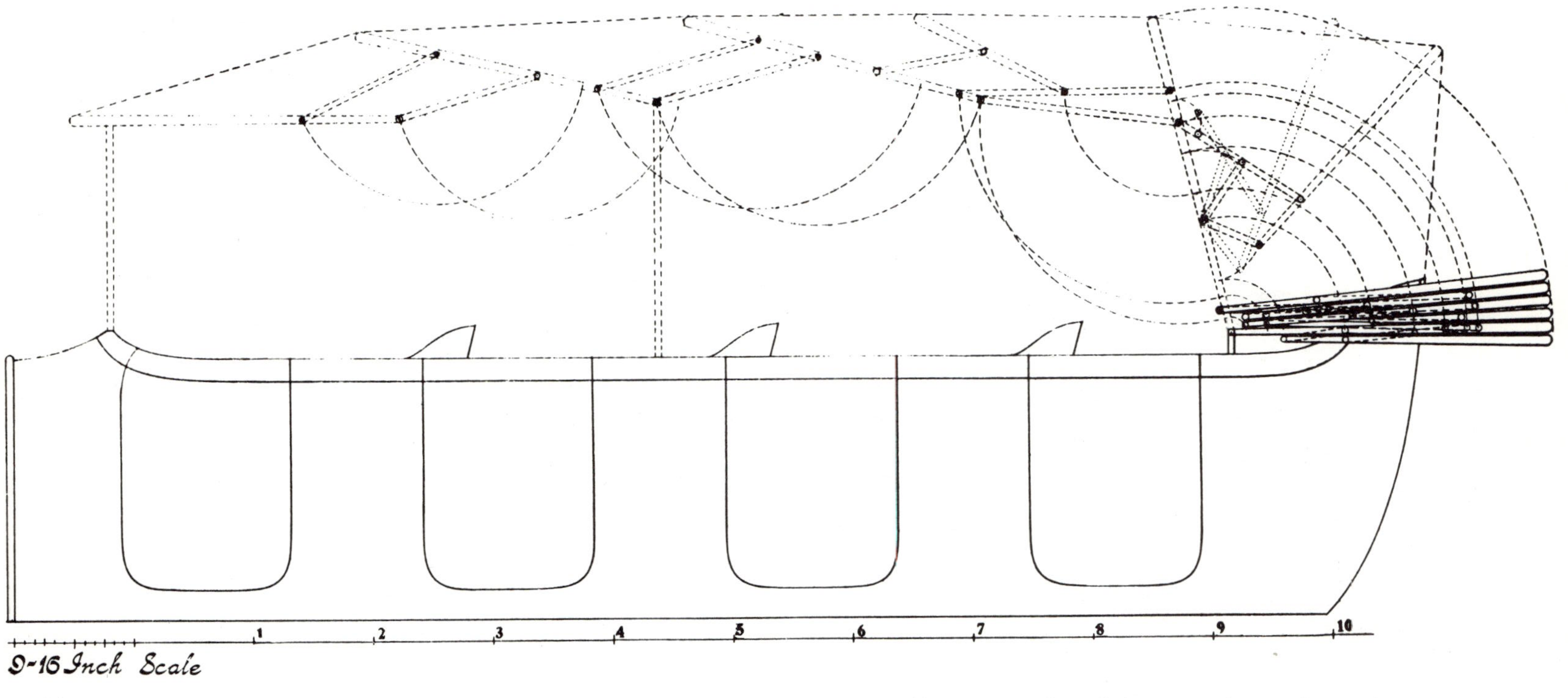

Fig. 10.—Note the movement of this top and especially the back part of top. The construction of these tops is very interesting.

The "One-Man" Top

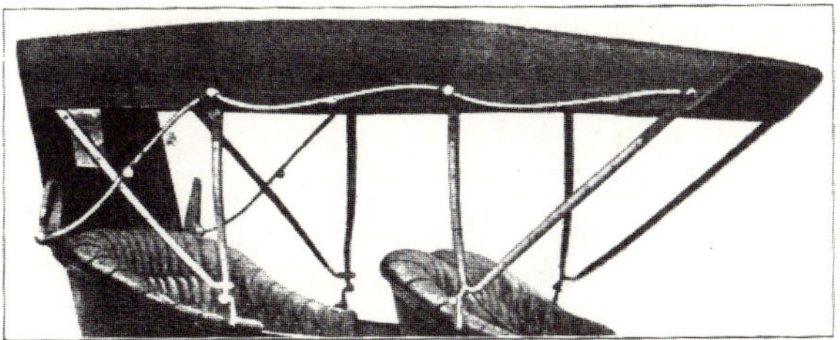

Four-bow extension-top

Since the building of the earlier passenger automobiles the well known "extension tops" have disappeared, and the "one-man" tops have taken their place; consequently they are not regarded at the present time as a novelty, but as a matter of fact one of the most essential accessories for the open automobile.

The well-constructed "one-man" top at the present time corresponds not only to what its name implies, but represents a consummation of style, harmony and convenience to the occupants. The importance of acquiring the correct construction, and also the most suitable finish, is nevertheless sometimes neglected; therefore, the necessity that a top should contribute toward the elegance and grace of a car and add further merit to its mechanical construction and its finish, is overlooked. The great possibilities of open car tops have been realized only during the past few years, and with their development it has been noted that automobile top builders who have adopted the improved top have derived a real benefit.

One of the recent tendencies in top construction is the increased use of slat irons, in place of the conventional black steel sockets. On these tops the long shanks on the wood bows are exposed and permit a variety of finishes on the wood and metal parts.

In the construction referred to these essential points merit consideration: Strength, durability, simplicity, ease of operation in raising and lowering the top, and its compactness when closed. The two most widely used tops are shown in the illustrations, type 15 and type 66, made by the Golde Patent Mfg. Co., this concern being the pioneers of the one-man top, introducing it more than ten years ago. It is, in its essential parts, the original top construction as has been used by all first-class automobile manufactures and top builders.

Type 66 has been adopted by the socket manufacturers as the type best adapted to the manufacture of bow sockets in large quantities at a reduced cost, and has been proven a great success. It has the advantage of being operated by the front bow, which forms a balanced unit in connection with the other bows. Type 66 has been until recently mostly used for bow sockets, but is now also used and manufactured in the slat iron equipment, and both of these types have been most successfully employed in the auto body trade.

The refinement displayed in high grade body work can readily be extended to the top when the slat iron equipment is used, and high-grade material is employed for the covering.

There are undoubtedly few parts where with small effort and expense such striking results can be obtained, an added effect to the body of custom-built cars of harmony and elegance. The slat irons are generally nickel-plated, and the long shanks, which are fitted to the bows, are finished in natural wood of any suitable color to match the rest of the finish. Mahogany and walnut in light and dark shades have been preferred; but the woods must be always in harmony with the body colors. When the top is down the effect is enhanced if the sleeves of the dust covers are made short.

"One-man" tops are universally built, but in no country has the development of slat iron "one-man" tops been so rapid and brought to such a high grade of perfection of workmanship and finish as by the automobile top trimmers of the United States.

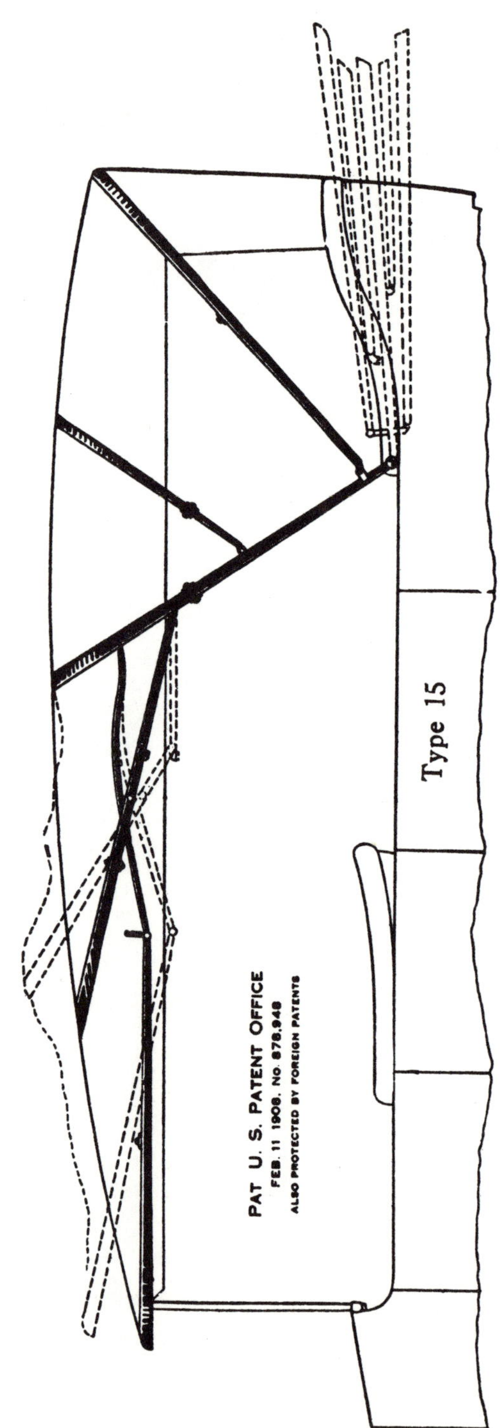

Type 15 is one of the original top constructions and has been used for the last ten years.

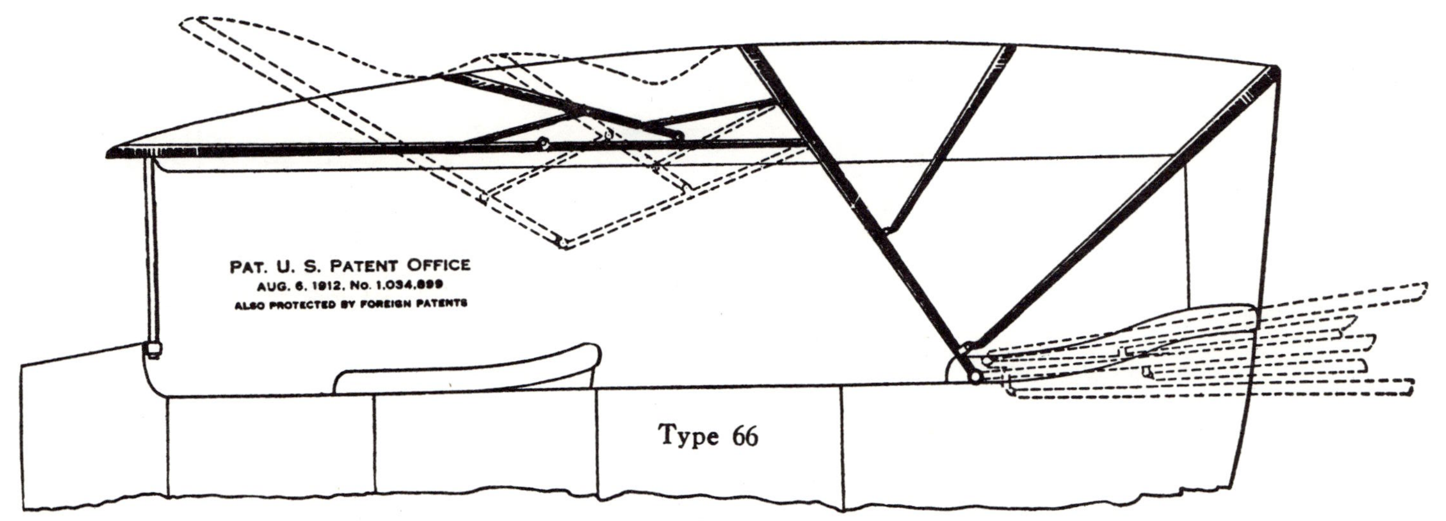

Type 66 has been adopted by the socket manufacturers as the type best adapted to the manufacture of bow sockets in large quantities, at a reduced cost.

A collapsible top is used on the greater number of the automobiles of today, and while there is an ever-increasing demand for the closed type car, the touring car, with a folding top, still retains its popularity. A folding top on a car gives a freedom to the passengers that is second only to being out walking, and when country travel is indulged in in fine weather, the pleasures are greatly increased if the top can be folded away, giving an unobstructed view in all directions.

The first tops used on the automobile were adaptations from the horse-vehicle tops, and as the automobile tops were long, curtains had to be used on the sides of the top to afford proper protection.

the chassis or body. These straps are pulled up tight so that the covering will be well stretched and so make a smooth appearing top.

To close the top down, the front sockets have to be taken off the body iron and attached to the front member of the rear socket. This is accomplished by having a bracket attached to the sockets that has a hole in it the same size as the front body iron has. The pin on the end of the front socket will then fit into this at the rear, the same cotter pin being used to hold it in position as is used when the top is in its open position. This is shown very plainly in Fig. 268. To operate this top successfully it was necessary to have one person on each side

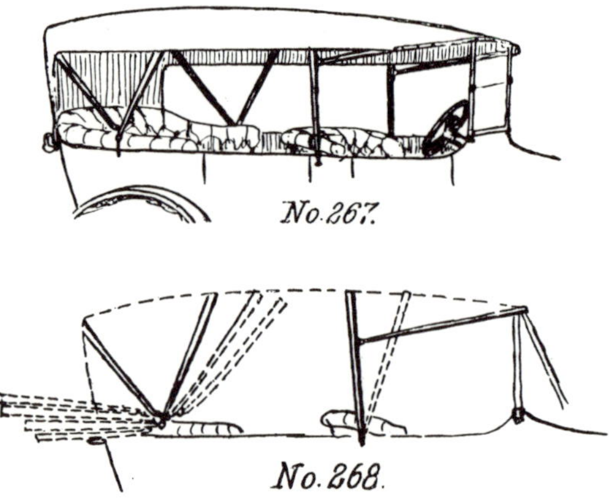

No. 267.

No. 268.

The top shown in Fig. 267 is a typical design of top that was commonly used previous to the adoption of the "one-man" type. The top illustrated in Fig. 267 consists of two front socket assemblies, right and left, and two rear assemblies, right and left. These sockets are made of steel and so shaped as to accommodate the wood bows that are driven into them.

In this top four bows are used. The front and rear sockets are set on to the top irons provided on the body. A waterproof cover is laid over the top of the bows and then stretched tight by attaching the rear bow to the back of the body by two straps, and at the front two straps run from the front bow to convenient places on

of the car. Each person would take hold of a front socket so that it would be raised or lowered evenly. On a large top it was difficult for even two men to manage. If a sudden storm came up the chances were that the passengers would be thoroughly wet before they could get the top up.

In order to overcome these objectionable features socket constructions were worked out where the front end was supported by suitable members from the rear bows. The front members were so designed that they would balance one another when the operation of raising or lowering the top was performed. The theory was that one person should be able to raise or lower the top while in the car.

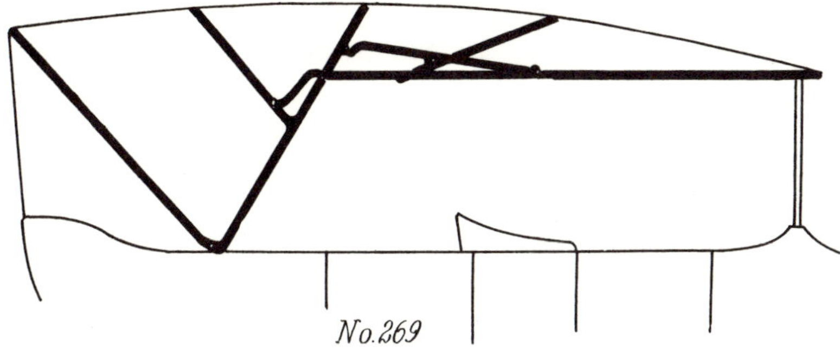

No. 269

In the first designs of this "one-man" type top the construction was prone to run to a good many levers and cables, which gave trouble by catching in the cloth and getting tangled up in operation. When the construction was developed to work easily it was found difficult to get the desired outline on the top, as the lever and bars had to maintain certain definite relations to one another.

To meet the conditions demanded, further movements had to be developed and the parts simplified. This has resulted in the type of sockets that are now used most generally. In Figs. 269, 270 and 271 are shown three typical layouts for sockets. They are all used very extensively. It will be seen that they all have a truss construction with the covering forming the tension cords. The rear end is anchored by straps to the back of the body while the front end is secured fast to the windshield. The top shown in Fig. 269 is claimed by the manufacturers to work easy by reason of the bell crank ends. It makes a very well-shaped top and folds very neatly.

The top illustrated in Figs. 272 and 273 has a socket which has recently been developed. It has a spring inserted inside one of the tubes. This spring applies pressure through the levers and members so that the operation of raising and lowering the top are assisted to a great extent. This spring makes the top almost automatic, as it raises the top and also prevents it dropping too quickly when it is let down. This principle applied to a long and heavy top makes its operation easy to a remarkable degree.

When an automobile top is designed there are a number of conditions that have to be considered, and these are outlined in the following:

The first factor is to decide what head clearance is desired. This is determined by the distance from the cushion to the point in the top that will come directly above the passenger's head. This is shown in Fig. 274, where a dimension B for the front seat calls for 38-38½, while on the rear seat the letter (A) is from 38 to 40. It can be estimated that the cushion will compress

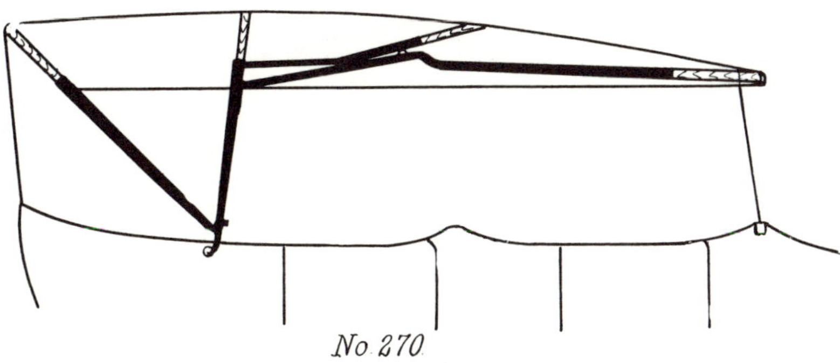

No. 270

111

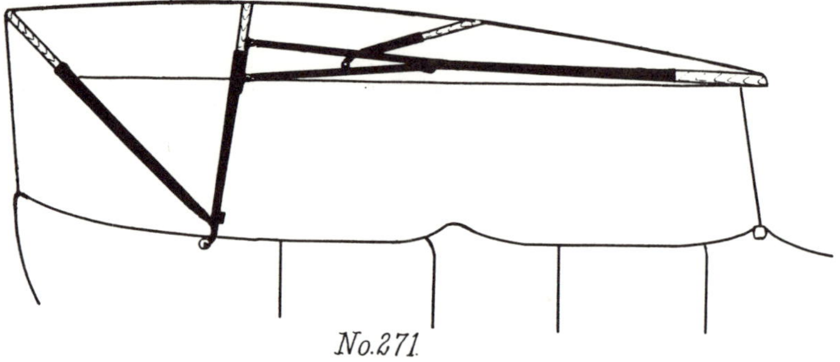

No.271.

at least 1 inch when the passengers are on it, but if the cushion is an extra soft one and allows the passengers to sink in deeper, the necessary allowance should be made.

The windshield height is the next thing to be decided upon, as the height of the windshield determines the amount of road vision the driver and passengers will have. The trend of design is to get the top as low as possible and also have the windshield short, but these should not be brought down too low, otherwise the driver's and passengers' vision will be obstructed. With these points established the outline of the top can be laid in. The back is set in the desired relation to the body line and at the front the line will terminate to suit the windshield.

The shape desired at the front and rear are taken up next, and as the back presents the larger surface to the eye it will be worked out first. The shape of the back bow and the height at which it sets determines the appearance of the back, so the bow outline is laid in as desired. The other

bows are so shaped that they will carry a uniform degree of outline throughout the complete length of the top. The importance of the shape of the top when it is up has been emphasized and the next consideration is to insure that it has the correct shape when it is folded or let down. The bows must be wide enough to clear the body and they should not project too far at the rear of the body. The line that the top is set in when it is folded should conform to the general lines of the body design. It is common practice to carry the spare tire at the rear, and when this is the case care has to be exercised to see that there are no bows setting over the tire so it would interfere with getting the tire on and off the tire carrier.

No.273.

The best way to arrive at satisfactory results is to make a preliminary layout and

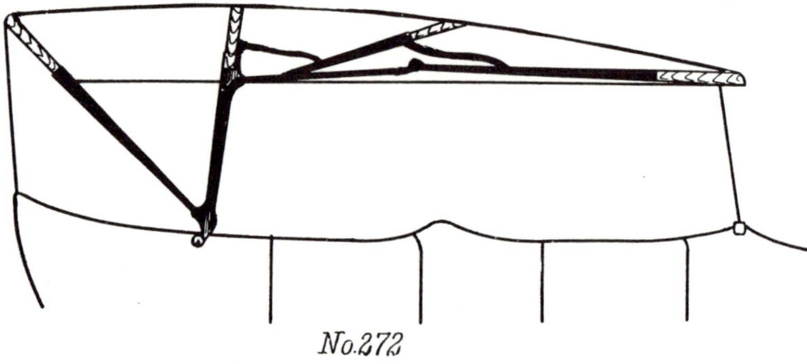

No.272

112

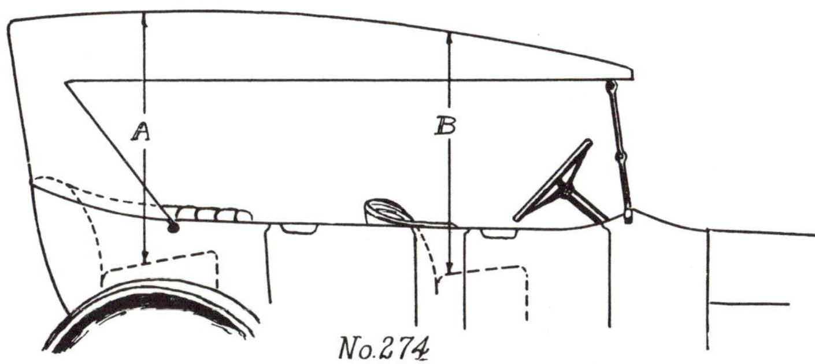

No.274

then submit this to the company which is to make the sockets, and as there are peculiarities in each socket manufacturer's constructions, it is advisable to have them go over the design and see if their constructions can be adapted to the requirements.

No.275.

The bows used are made from ash or oak, which is machined and bent to the shapes required. While various sized sections are used, the 1½ by 1 is the most popular. The ends that are to be driven into the sockets are shaved off so that they will conform to the taper end of the socket, as shown in Fig. 275. In specifying the shape of the bow to the bowmaker, the width, height, section, radius and crown are required. The dimensions A, B, C, D and E required are shown in Fig. 276, and when they are given in the same manner as shown the bow-maker will have no trouble in understanding the requirements.

The different sections shown in Fig. 277, A, B, C and D, give a good idea of the shapes that are required for the bows used at different parts of the top. These sections show the corners of the bows removed on the edge or edges that come in contact with the covering. If these corners were left sharp the edges in time would cut through the top material. In Fig. 278 is shown how these corners set in the top.

The use of a tubular socket is standard American practice. The European practice is to use a flat iron construction and the bows

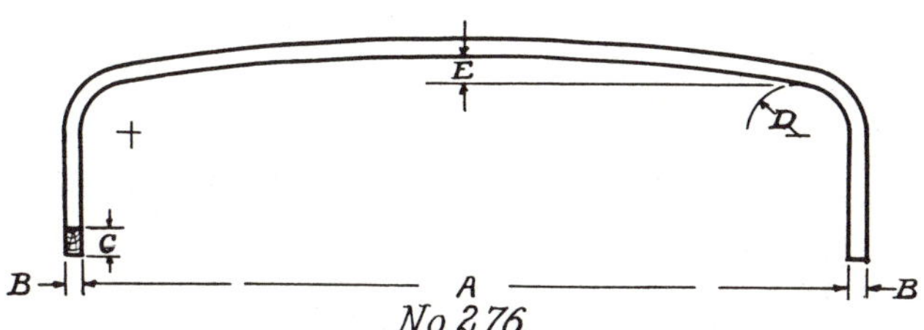

No.276.

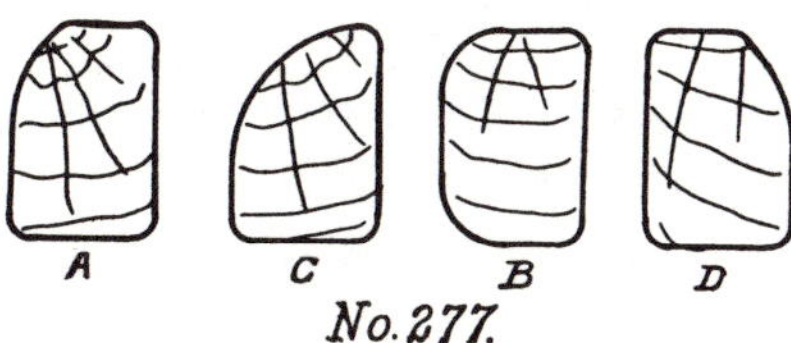

No.277.

are attached by wood screws. By making the top construction this way the parts are made slightly smaller and in some cases neater, but the cost and time required to make them offset any advantages they may possess.

On the front bow a suitable fastener has to be attached to secure the top to the windshield, and as there are several different

113

No. 278

methods used to do this it will be interesting to review them. The most common type of fastener is one similar to that shown in Fig. 279, which consists of a malleable iron bracket with a screw that has a convenient shaped head, preferably with winged extensions. A sectional view in Fig. 280 shows how this set screw engages with the pin

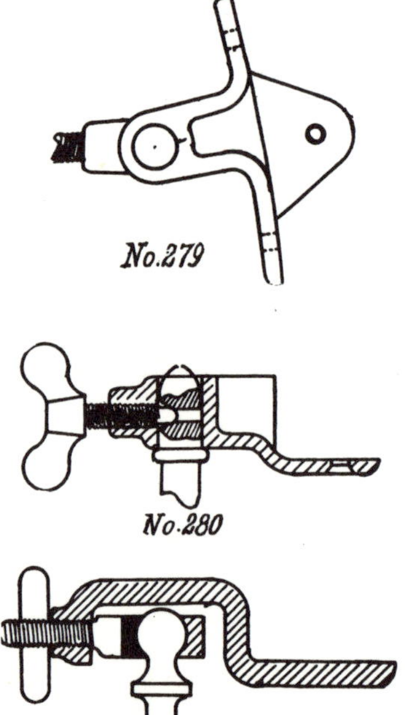

No. 279

shown in the sectional view. To disengage the top this slide is pushed inward, which disengages the slide from the windshield post, leaving the top free to rise. This is a very simple arrangement and when it is properly fitted works in a satisfactory manner.

The back bow has to be braced in position by back brace straps. There are several ways of arranging these straps; some of these methods will be described.

The first method is to use a double strap that is looped into a suitable fastener. The loose ends of the strap are nailed to the bow as shown in Fig. 283a. The second method is to attach the straps to the top of the bow and let them come down over the inside of the bow as shown in Fig. 284. The third method is to use a single strap with a buckle to allow for adjustment as shown in Fig. 285. A fourth style, shown in Fig. 286, is to use a double end of strap that is Y-shaped

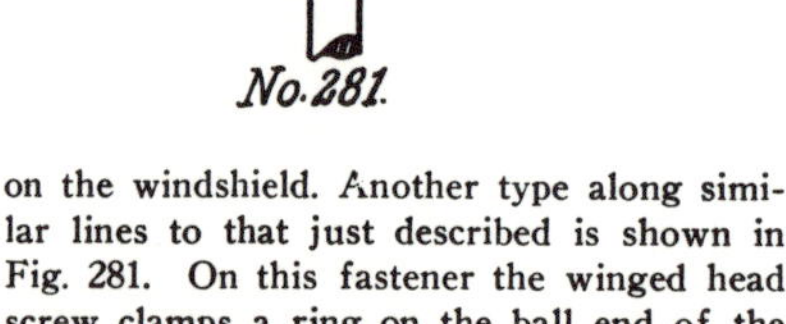

No. 280

No. 281.

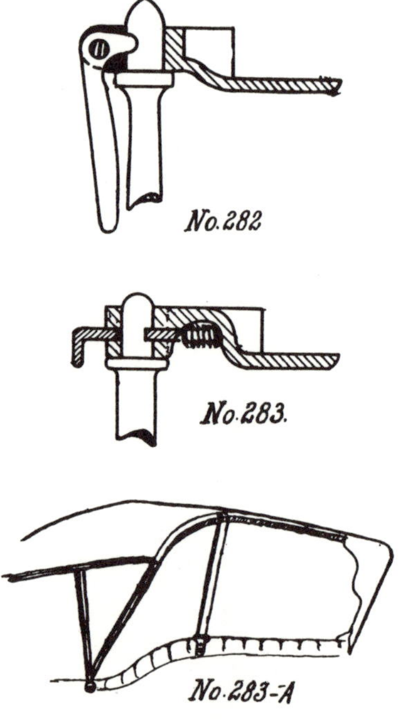

No. 282

No. 283.

No. 283-A

on the windshield. Another type along similar lines to that just described is shown in Fig. 281. On this fastener the winged head screw clamps a ring on the ball end of the shield.

In Fig. 282 is shown a toggle lever arrangement for clamping the top to the shield. The fastener shown in Fig. 283 is a semi-automatic, as the slide is operated by a spring that pushes the slide ahead and into a slot that is located on the windshield bracket and

114

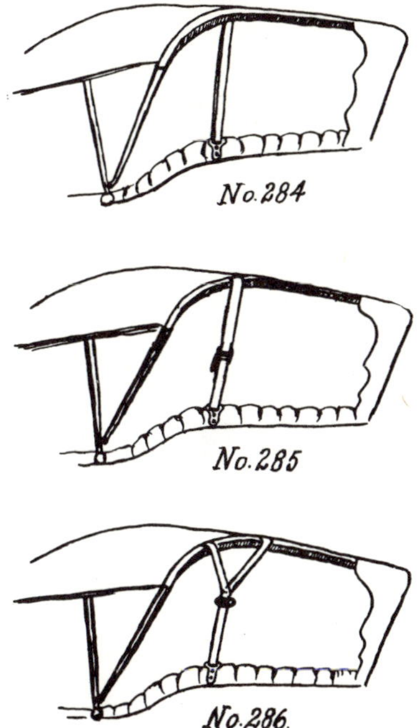

No. 284

No. 285

No. 286.

passengers to a great extent from the dust. In the design shown in Fig. 290 these gypsy sides are extensions of the back curtain. There is another method of making these, and that is to put small, separate triangular curtains in and fasten them to the back curtain and bow socket as shown in Fig. 291. While this is not as good a job as making them integral with the back curtain, they answer the purpose very well in providing protection.

A suitable light has to be provided in the back curtain and this may take any one of a great variety of shapes. In Figs. 292 to 300 are shown a variety of designs for back lights, which give a very good representation of the different manufacturers' ideas. A back light of liberal proportions is desirable for the driver's convenience, and as these lights are usually made of pyralin, which is a cellulose composition, it is better to have several small lights in preference to one large one, as a large one would be more liable to crack and break. On some of the higher priced cars and on large cars, a glass is inserted as shown in Fig. 301, instead of the pyralin. This, of course, requires a suitable framework to be constructed in the back to support it properly.

where it attaches to the bows. This can be fastened either to the inside or outside of the bow. Style number five, shown in Fig. 287, is to attach a loop to the bow and put either a leather strap or cotton strap through it and the fastener on the body, the ends of the strap to be fastened together with a suitable buckle.

The back and side curtains will next be described. The back curtain attaches to the top of the rear bow and to the back end of the body. It is generally made of one piece, the upper end being nailed in position and the joint it makes with the top cover is covered by a suitable molding, while the lower end is attached either by nailing or by suitable detachable fasteners as shown in Fig. 288. There are some designers who like to have the back curtain in three pieces, as shown in Fig. 289, in order to permit the center section to be raised in hot weather. The reason for raising this portion is to permit the air to pass right through the car and not have any back drafts.

Another style of back curtain which is largely used has extensions on each side that run to the back bow socket. These are called gypsy-curtains. They protect the rear

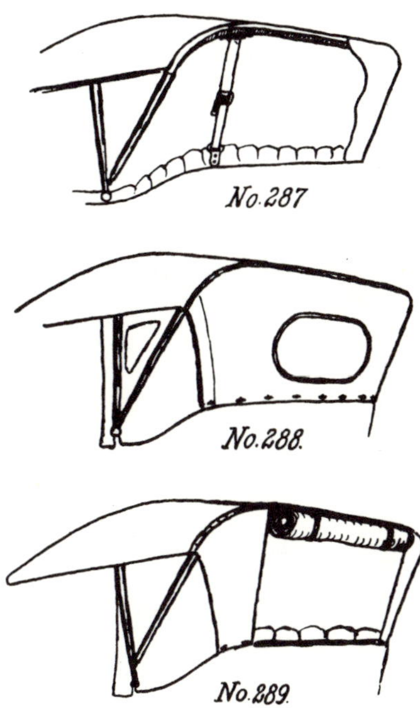

No. 287

No. 288.

No. 289.

115

The side curtains are made from a material to match the top covering and back curtains, and so arranged that they can be opened conveniently above the doors so that the passengers can get in and out. Suitable lights made of pyralin are provided and so arranged as to give a maximum amount of vision for the passengers. There are two arrangements of side curtains covered by pat-

Fig. 304. As each of the three curtains is of a different shape a lot of time is saved in putting them up when they are located by these loops and straps, as without any locating straps it takes quite a little time and trouble to sort out the curtains when it is desired to put them up.

In order to attach these curtains to the top suitable, quick detachable fasteners have to

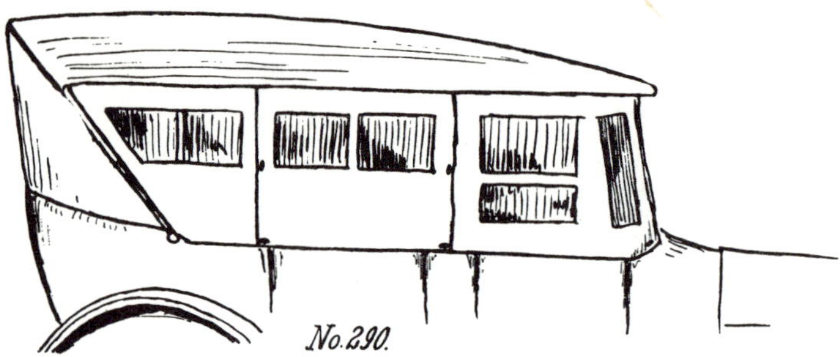

No. 290.

ents called the "jiffy" and the "Collins," both of which are used extensively. The jiffy style of side curtain is shown in Fig. 302. The material is so sewn together that it will quickly fold up into a compact space. A cable is provided inside the top and the curtains are strung on to it, so that a movement ahead or backward folds or unfolds the curtain very easily. The curtains are usually divided into three sections on each side, and when they are not in use they fold up and fasten on to the top bows by

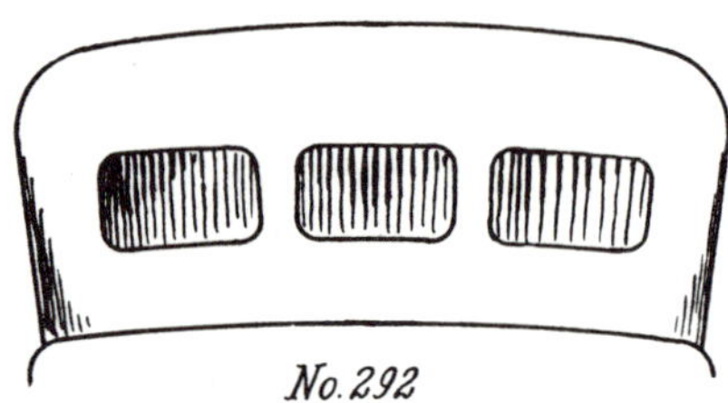

No. 292

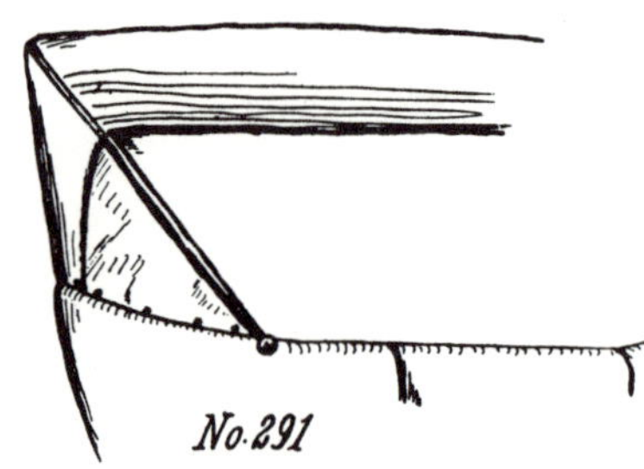

No. 291

straps, the right and left section folding together at each place. This is shown in Fig. 303.

The Collins system, as shown in Fig. 290, provides a small wire loop, for the curtain to be attached to, the idea being to keep the curtains located adjacent to the part of the top and body that they attach to. See

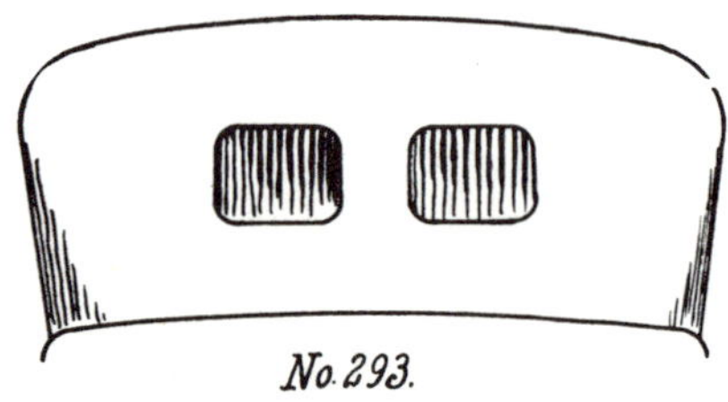

No. 293.

No. 294

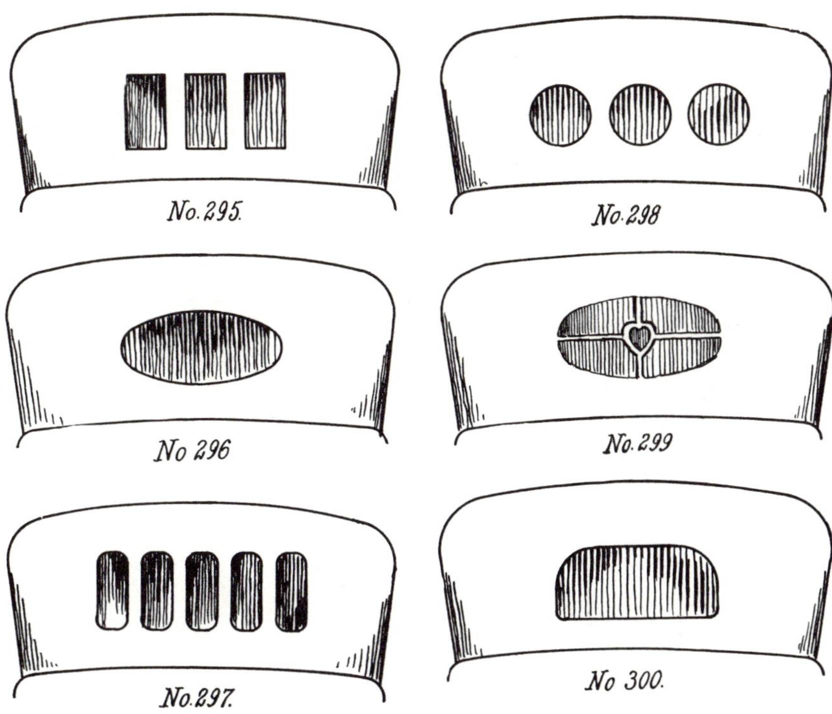

No. 295.   No. 298

No 296   No. 299

No. 297.   No 300.

be used and a brief description of these will prove interesting. A fastener of a type widely used is shown in Figs. 305 to 309. Fig. 305 shows the fastener used when it has to be attached to the solid part of the body or top, and as it is seen is attached by two screws. This, and all the styles, are made in what is called double and single type. The single type is for use where only one thickness of cloth is to be attached to it, while the double will take two thicknesses.

The eyelet and plate shown in Fig. 310 are the parts that attach to the cloth. The prongs are clinched down over the plate as shown in Fig. 311. The type shown in Fig 306 has a wood screw end on it for use when it is desired to screw it into the wood, while that shown in Fig. 307 has a metal thread for screwing on to a metal section. In Fig. 308 the fastener has a plain stud on it. This is used where it is desired to rivet it to a plate. A type to attach to cloth is shown in Fig. 309. This has two prongs which fasten over a plate as shown. The Murphy type of fastener is in operation at right angles to its normal position as shown in

Figs. 312 and 313. Fig. 312 shows the fastener in position in an eyelet; in Fig. 313 it shows the head turned and locking it in position.

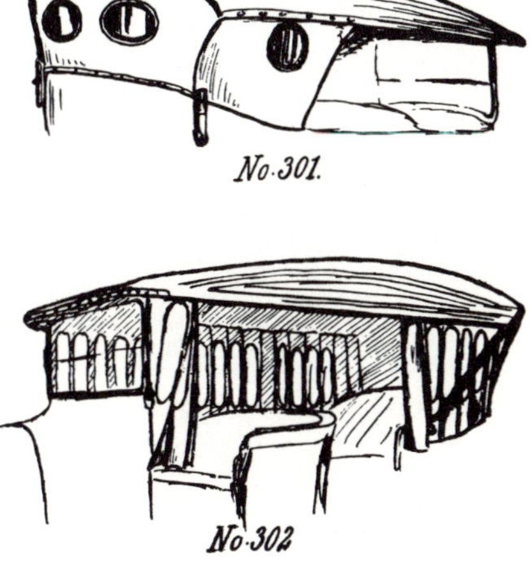

No. 301.

No. 302

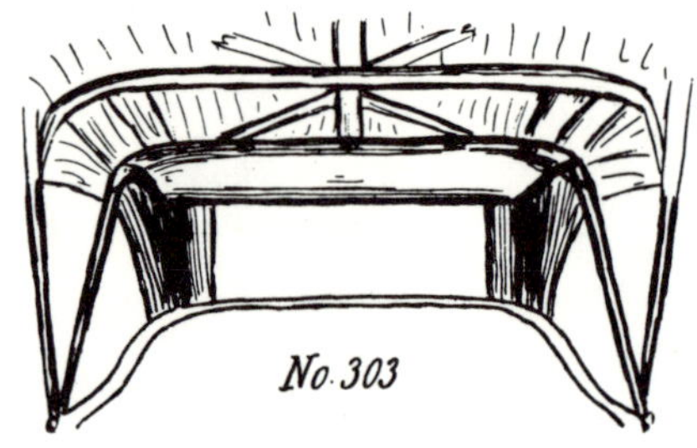

No. 303

pockets in position as shown in Fig. 320. The rest is attached to an iron which projects from the body. A top holder that is now in general use is called the Bair top holder. This consists of two main malleable iron sections with a suitable lever on the top which clamps the main section tight on to the bows and holds them securely in position. In Fig. 321 is shown this holder in position and the dotted lines show it partially open. The holder attaches to an iron which projects from the body.

No. 304.   No. 305   No. 306   No. 307   No. 308.   No. 309   No. 310

While the catch portions of the various makes of fasteners is different, the back portions that attach to the various parts are similar to constructions described in the Murphy. The "lift the dot" fastener is one used very extensively and can be adapted to practically any conditions. They are made with the different backs to suit the part they are to be used with. In Fig. 314 is shown the main portions of this type of fastener. The catch part has a small wire spring in it that snaps over the ball-shaped end of the other portion. The stud is attached to one part and the fastener to the other part that is to be fastened. It will be seen that a plate and prongs are provided to clinch over the material.

The Carr glove fastener is used a great deal on parts of the top and side curtains. These fasteners are made to attache to the cloth on wood and in metal. The principle of their construction is shown in Fig. 315. This is made of three parts—a cap, clasp and stud. The cap has an extension that clinches over the clasp portion. The clasp has a small wire spring in it that snaps over the stud when it is engaged. The Church fastener is shown in Fig. 316. By depressing the small knob it permits the curtain to be removed. There are three parts, the catch, plate and washer, shown in Figs. 317, 318 and 319, respectively. This construction is very ingenious and positive in action.

When the top is folded, a suitable method of holding it securely in position has to be used. The earlier method was to strap the

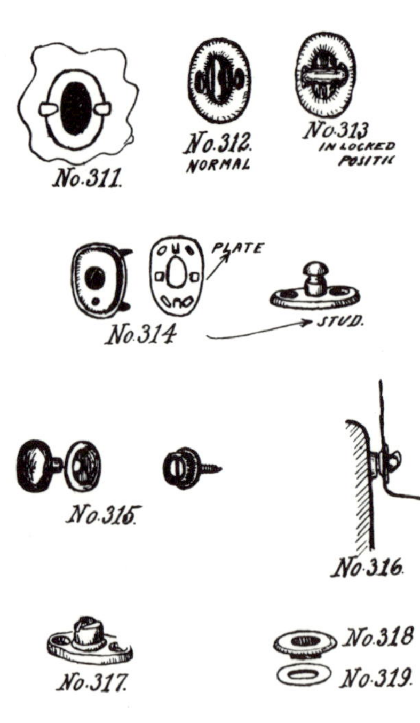

There are a number of different styles of holders on the market besides those described, but they are not used as extensively as the Bair type, so they will not be taken up at this time.

118

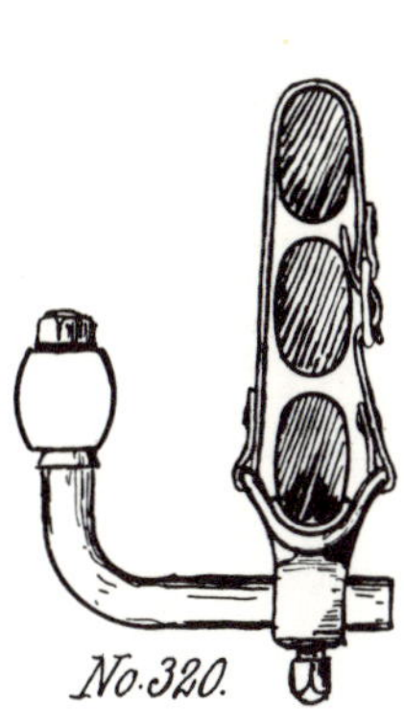

No. 320.

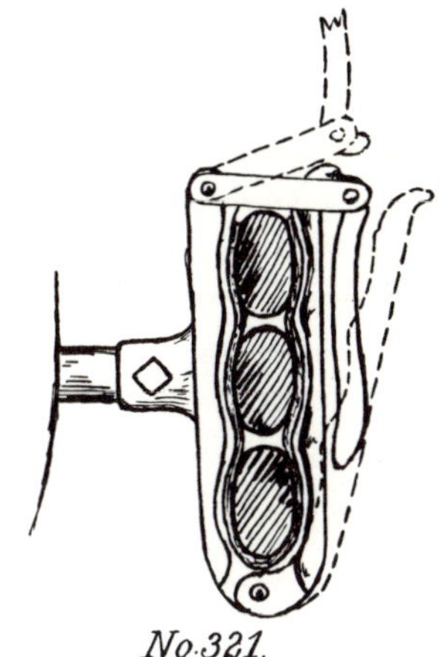

No. 321.

With the top folded it is necessary to provide a cover to keep the dust from collecting in it. The cover used is called a "top boot" and is made from a cloth similar to that used on the top covering. The boot is made to fit snugly over the sockets and extends as far as the trimmings on the seat back. In order to hold it in position two or more straps are fastened to the front upper edge and two or more to the front lower edge. These straps pull down over the seat trimming, and are secured to the seat frame under the cushion, as shown in Fig. 322. In order to make a neat appearance on the sides two extensions can be provided that run to the nut on the top iron. A fastener is located on this which helps to hold it in position.

The standard type of top has been described in most of its phases. There is another design that deserves some comments and that is the top that is constructed to fold into a compartment in the back of the body. There is (or was, at least) one manufacturer who is supplying a top of this kind as regular equipment. In order to make a satisfactory installation of this type of top, the body has to be specially constructed, and the general design adaptable to it. In Fig. 323 is shown a car design that has them worked out to get these results. It will be noted that there is no visible evidence of the top when it is folded away, as it is on the car illustrated.

Another type of body that has a compartment for a top is shown in Fig. 324. The lines show the general construction of the top. It will be seen that the lines and shape of the top are different from the regular car top. This is caused by the conditions that have to be worked out to make the top fold close to the body and so keep the compartment from getting too large or cumbersome. The advantage of a top of this type is the protection that the top gets from dust; it also does away with cloth covers and loose flaps, and in some cases it is possible to raise and lower the top quicker as the top holders, top cover and socket holders do not have to be manipulated. The disadvantages are that the shape of the top is not as good

No. 322

No. 323.

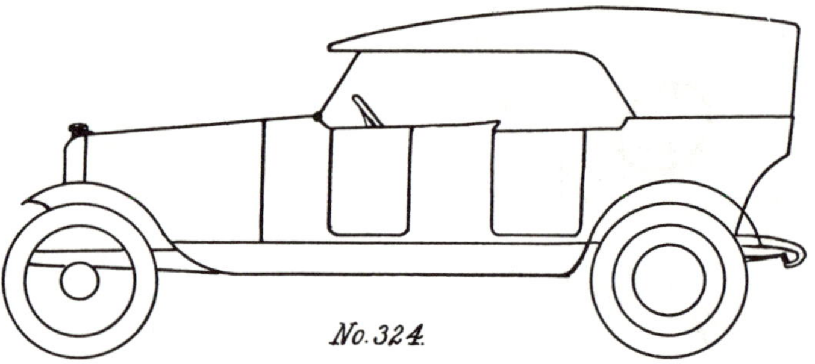

No. 324.

as the regular type and that the body construction is complicated and the lines of the car are changed by the addition of the compartment.

The Victoria top is quite popular on cars for use in the city, as it has a striking appearance and is very adaptable for city use. The construction is identical to those tops that were used on carriages. The general form of construction is to use from three to five bows with outside joint irons to hold it in position, as shown in Fig. 325. The object of the design is to have a top that affords protection from the sun, and it does not obstruct the vision as much as a regular top does. It is also possible to fold it down when an open car is desired, and then it has the appearance of a regular folded top. The best grade of leather is generally used to cover the top. It is not advisable to fold it down, as the leather will crack or show the line of the fold, and for this reason these tops are not folded very often.

To afford proper protection in case of rain an extension curtain is provided that will attach to the windshield, and then provision is made for side curtains. This is shown in Fig. 325.

There are two methods of building these tops. One is what is termed a shifting rail and the other is where the top is built so that the covering fastens to the body. The shifting rail type has a rail that fastens to the body, the top covering being fastened to it. This permits the top being taken right off the body. When this shifting rail is used the rail makes the top project over the sides of the body. This has a tendency to make the top appear larger, as shown in the illustration in Fig. 325. For this reason it does not look as well as the top that is built on to the body. The increasing popularity of the Victoria top has caused manufacturers to devise a top construction that is solid, eliminating the joint iron so that it can not be folded, and then setting a fancy

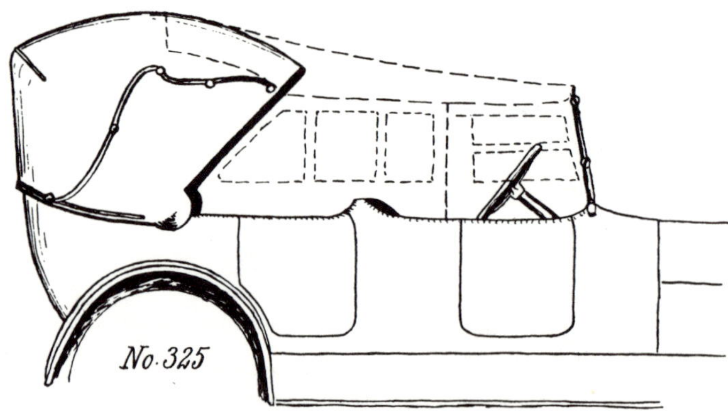

No. 325

No·326.

shaped glass in the sides as shown in Fig. 326. This gives a Victoria effect, but with smooth lines and simpler construction.

The winter top is a construction that has been developed to afford more protection to passengers in the winter, and as the automobile is being used, to a great extent, all the year round, the detachable winter top construction is being used quite extensively. The winter top virtually converts a touring car into a closed car. There are a number of well-constructed tops on the market that make a very convenient adaptation for winter use.

One manufacturer has made a specialty of a detachable top on his cars for several years. The body is especially arranged so that the top can be fitted very easily. This top and the details of the attachment are shown in Fig. 327. A great variety of winter tops have been marketed of various designs. Unfortunately the majority of them were very crudely constructed, and they did a great deal towards retarding the development of this business. From these early attempts there has evolved a top that is now proving satisfactory and acceptable. See Figs. 328, 329 and 330.

A brief description of a type of top now being used will be given. The top consists of a wood framework with composition or metal panels, sides and roof. The composition panel is generally used, and this is covered with a good grade of imitation leather. The top, back and side quarters are attached together and fastened to the windshield at the front, and to the rear top iron at the rear. The rear side glasses are set in a permanent frame which is attached to the top and body by small steel plates. The center posts from which the upper part of the door swings are fastened to the body and top by suitable steel plates. The upper sections of the door hinges from the top posts are attached to the top of the car door. A handle

No·327

No. 328.

is provided in this upper section to operate the door from the outside. This has an extension on it on the inside that attaches to the regular door lock handle. This device is necessary, as the majority of automobiles have the door lock handles on the inside of the doors.

The glasses in the doors are constructed so that the upper half can be lowered when desired, as shown in Fig. 329. On some of the winter tops they are arranged so that the upper door frames, side posts and rear quarters can be removed for summer use, giving a "Springfield" effect, and to provide against sudden storms a set of side curtains are fitted. These fold up and set in a pocket in the top lining.

No. 329

No. 330

BY KINGSTON FORBES, M. E.

Assistant Body Engineer, Buick Motor Car Co., Member Society of Automotive Engineers.

Top Work on Open Cars
How to Repair a Top

ATTENDANT with the growth of the automobile industry, specialized service stations for repairing electrical systems, radiators, bodies, etc., have sprung up, and have formed a legitimate branch of the business. Repairshops specializing in top repair likewise fill a definite need, and either as a separate business or a department of a service station, should show a fair profit.

But a small amount of equipment is necessary in a top repairshop, and this, with the exception of the sewing machines, may be made by the repairman himself. The shop layout is shown in Fig. 1, and it will be noted that the mechanic can go from the car to the lay-

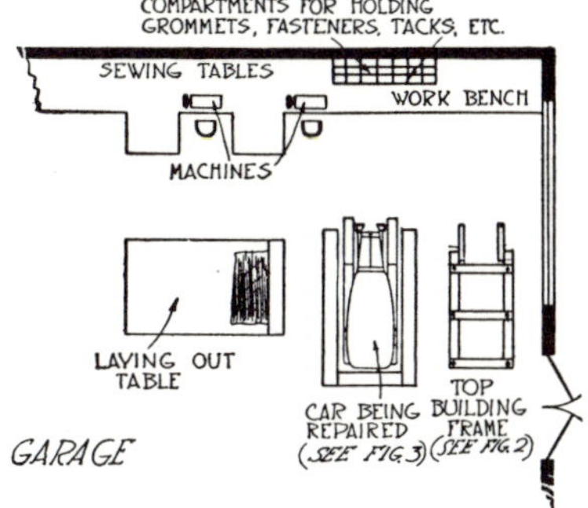

Fig. 1—The above layout permits the workman to work with a minimum of lost time

ing out table or the machines with a minimum of movement. This is essential, as profits will largely depend upon the efficiency with which the workmen operate.

The top building frame is shown in Fig. 2, and it is only used when the car for which the top is being repaired cannot be left during the work. It is simply an adjustable framework upon which the top may be placed in exactly the position it occupies when up, and on the car. For each car the frame is set to duplicate the measurements of the top supporting irons and the car body. Then the workman can repair or rebuild the top with assurance that it will fit when returned to the car. *But when possible, the top should be left on the car during the repair.*

In order to render all parts of the top accessible, when left on the car, a framework shown in Fig. 3 is set up around three sides of the car. This framework is about 18 in. high, and comprises three planks resting on four small wooden horses. Another method of accomplishing the same result, yet one which the author has never seen, would be to construct a pit below the floor level. This would permit the workman to work directly from the floor and save the time lost in stepping to and from the platform.

All work is laid out and cut on the laying out table shown in Fig. 4. This table is about 6 ft. wide, 12 ft. long and 28 in. high. A notched rack at one end supports the rolls of top material and enables the workman to readily obtain or replace the top material when desired. Rolls may be easily removed from the frame, or as many as three rolls of material may be carried at one time.

The tools of the workman are few, comprising a light cross pene hammer, with a tack puller fitted to the end of the handle; a heavy pair of shears, a small cold chisel and a nail set or punch. These are carried in a special apron, made of top material, as shown in Fig. 5. In addition, a carpenter's square, a 10-ft. straight edge, a yard stick and a plumb bob are required. The plumb bob is used to plumb up the edges of the back curtain, when fitting, to make certain that they are hung straight.

In addition, several special punches and dies will be necessary for cutting the openings for the curtain fasteners. One of these—styled the Murphy die—is shown in Fig. 7 and corresponding dies are used for each type of fastener.

The sewing machine used in this work is of extra heavy construction, and is similar to those used by harness makers. These machines should be motor-driven, and may be purchased from almost any reliable sewing machine manufacturer.

So much for the equipment—now for the method of doing the work. Briefly this consists of removing the top material, part by part, using the parts as patterns to cut the new parts by; fitting the parts to the top frame; removing the parts; sewing them together, and then placing them again on the frame. Careful work is essential, and after carefulness has become a habit speed may be developed. Carefulness, then speed, are the only two requirements for a successful top repairman.

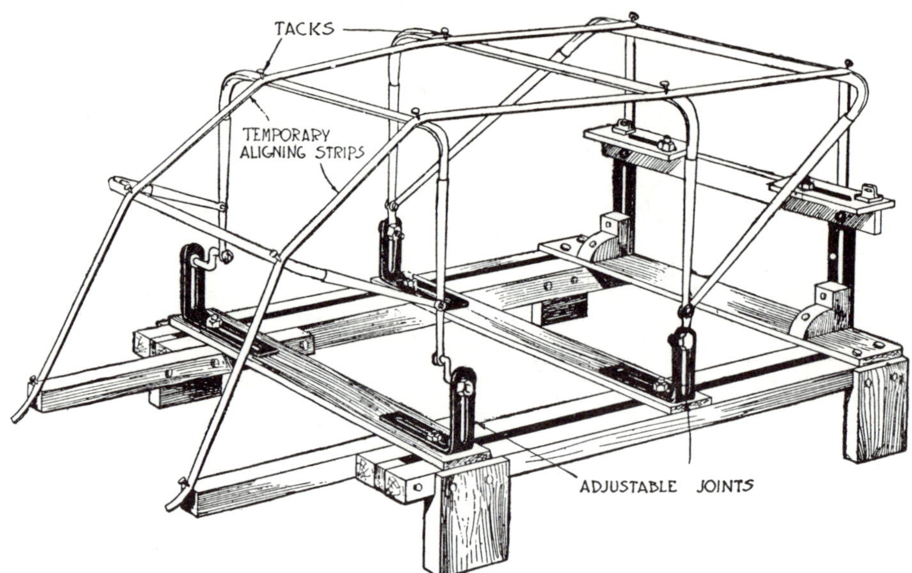

Fig. 2—When the car cannot be left in the shop, this adjustable frame enables the mechanic to duplicate the method of holding used on the car

The following is a typical example of the method used in re-covering an automobile top. Though it specifically applies to a Ford top, in general, it may be applied to any car.

1—Remove the top covering from the frame, part by part, using the hammer and cold chisel as tools. Note how each part is fastened, as the rebuilding must be exactly the reverse of the tearing down.

2—Using each part as a pattern, one by one, mark out the new parts on the top material. Care must be taken to allow extra material at the edges for fastening the material to the frame. The method of constructing the rear quarter is shown in Fig. 10, and this method applies in general to each of the top parts.

All metal fastener holes should be punched, using the holes in the old parts as guides, and all square corners should be checked up by means of the square. The parts are then sent to the machine, and the necessary sewing done. The celluloid windows are also placed in the rear curtain at this time.

In the meantime the top frame should be placed in good condition. If any bows are broken new bows should be fitted. Ordinarily new wrapping should

be tacked around the bows, but if this wrapping is only faded, it may be dyed to conform to the inside of the top material.

3—The side pad covers should now be made, according to the pattern shown in Fig. 8. On the Ford black cambric is used, but in every case the material should conform in color and quality to that used in the top material.

4—Line up the top bows. The method of doing this is shown in Fig. 2. Heavy canvas straps are passed over each side of the bows, drawn tight, and tacked in place. The front bow should fit down over the windshield; the two middle bows should be vertical, and the position of the rear bow can be gaged by the length of the straps holding it down to the body back.

5—The side pad liners are next tacked in place and the burlap strips tacked tightly in place. After this the curled hair, or cotton packing, is replaced, and the side pad flaps pasted into place. If desired, the edges of the pad may be sewed together. The above operations are shown in detail in Fig. 9.

6—The rear quarters and back curtain are now fitted and tacked in place, after the metal fasteners have been applied, as shown in Fig. 7. All vertical

124

Fig. 3—Most tops are repaired right on the car, and a framework on three sides of the car renders all parts accessible

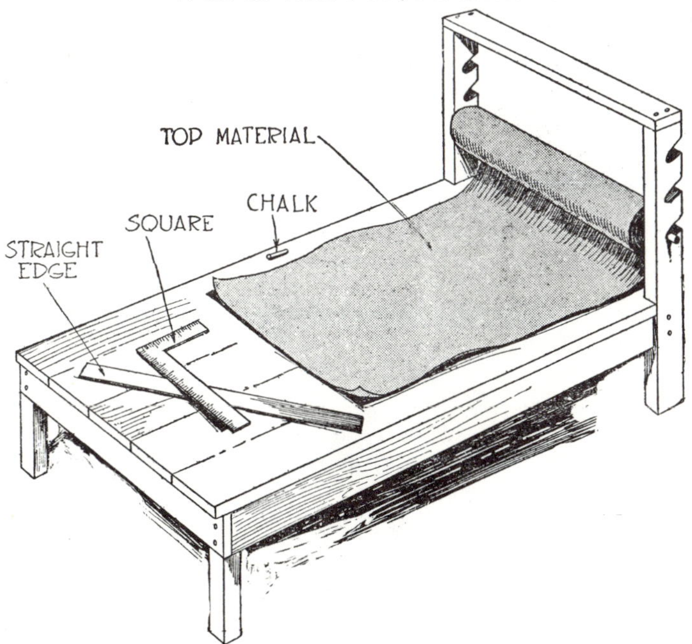

Fig. 4—The rolls of top material are carried on rods hung in a notched upright, and the material is marked out and cut to form on the laying out table

edges are plumbed up with a plumb bob, as any edge out of the vertical here is particularly noticeable.

7—The two side quarters are now temporarily tacked in place, beginning at the front and working to the back. These quarters should be drawn tight, without wrinkling. The edges of the deck are then turned under, and the deck is temporarily tacked in place.

8—By carefully fitting and changing, the top may be fitted to the bows in exactly the position it is to occupy. When everything appears to fit correctly the side curtains should be placed in position, and if necessary, the tacks should be removed and the top pieces shifted until the side curtains fit. (*In most cases new side curtains do not have to*

be made; but if so, the new curtains should be fitted at this point.)

9—When everything is right the mating edges of the top pieces should be marked with chalk, and these marks crossmarked, as shown in Fig. 11. Then by joining the corresponding marks together, the sewing machine operator can

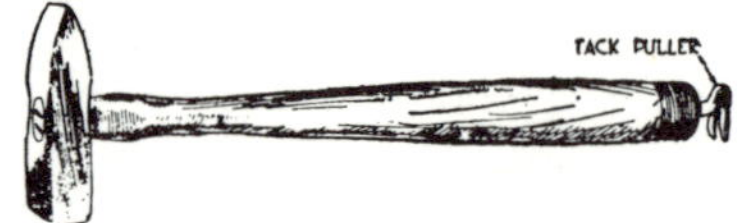

Fig. 6—The outer end of the hammer handle is fitted with a tack puller, thus combining the two tools

sew the parts together correctly. Chalk marks should also be placed at the points the edge of the top crosses the bows. This permits the top to be correctly replaced after a sewing.

10—The parts of the top are then removed, and the flaps on the edges that are to be sewed trimmed down to a width of about 2 in. The parts then are sent to the machine and sewed together.

11—To complete the work it is only necessary to replace the top covering and tack it securely in place. All extending edges are removed and the joints covered by a narrow strip of cloth material fastened by black upholstering tacks.

The above covers the method of completely replacing the top covering, with the exception of the side curtains. As stated, this is rarely necessary, as the side curtains are little used. If desired, any one part of the top may be replaced with new material, providing the other parts are in good condition. However, if either the deck or side quarters

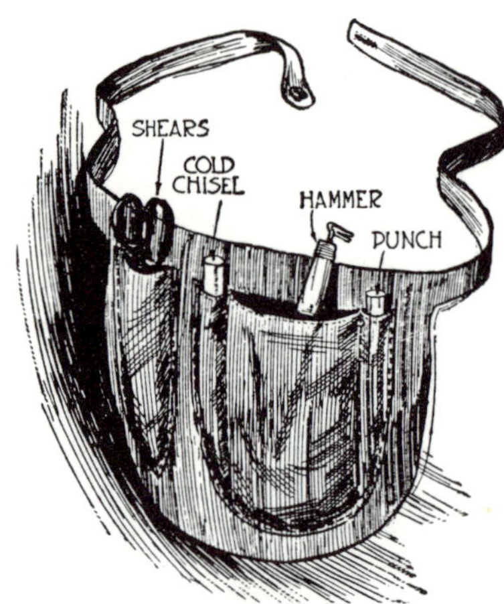

Fig. 5—An apron of top material carries all the tools commonly used by the top maker. Thereby no time is wasted in hunting for the desired tool

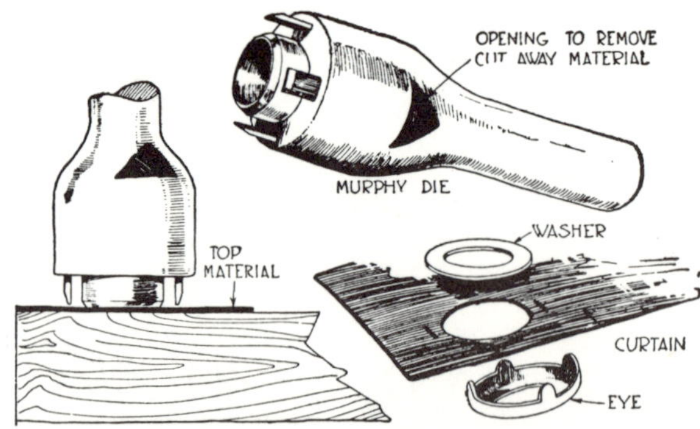

Fig. 7—Special dies are required to cut the openings for the fasteners. This is a most common type

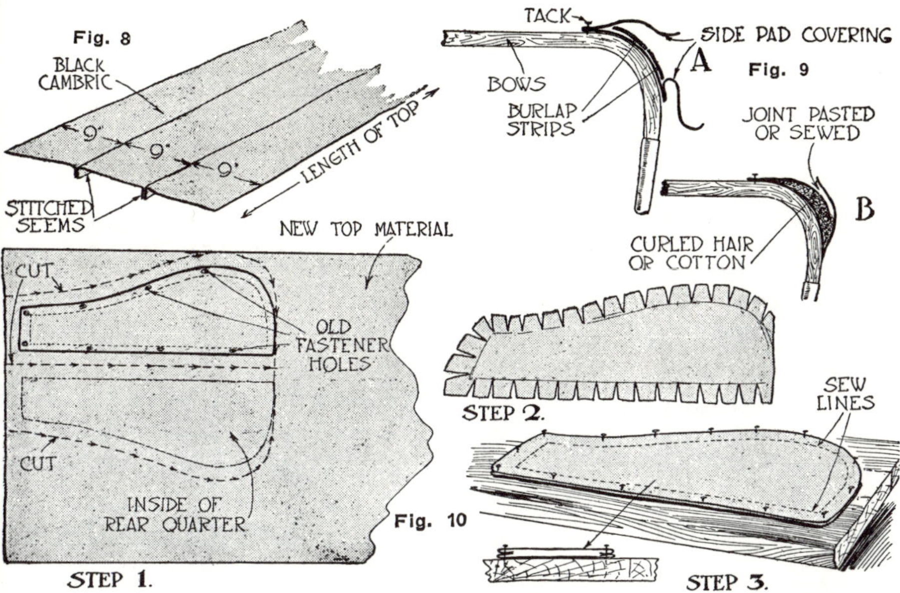

Fig. 8—The side pads are a single strip of cambric 29 In. wide, and sewed as shown. Fig. 9—This is the method of building up the side pads. Fig. 10—This shows the various steps in laying out and cutting a rear quarter. It is then taken to the machine and sewed

must be replaced, it is necessary to tear the top completely down in order to sew it together again.

Any repairshop, by the investment of a small amount of money in equipment, and the exertion of reasonable care, can develop a profitable top repair department. It is as an essential part of the trade as is the machine shop or the vulcanizing shop.

In cases where it is necessary to replace some parts of the top covering, it will usually be found advisable to renovate the interior and exterior of the balance of the covering to make it conform to the appearance of the new part.

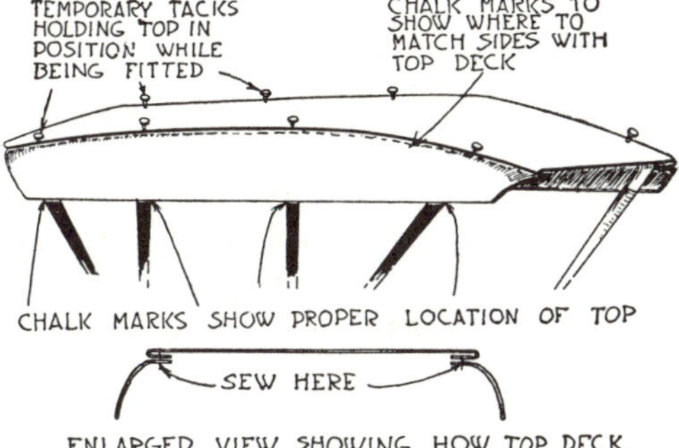

Fig. 11—After all parts of the top are made, they are temporarily tacked to the bows and fitted. When a perfect fit is secured, the edges are marked, and the parts removed and sewed. They may then be replaced on the frame and permanently fastened in place

Always Easiest to Operate---
Always the Most Sightly

THE owner of a "Jiffy quipt" car has the nearest approach to a truly "convertible" car that money can buy.

For "Jiffy" Curtains, fitting snug, tight and close afford absolute protection from the elements—and they always look good.

"Jiffy" Curtains shut out cold, rain or snow and are within quick, easy reach at all times. Handiest summer or winter.

"Jiffy" Curtains can be brought into action almost instantly. They slide into position on wire cables.

"Jiffy" Curtains can be stowed away just as easily. Simply slide them back on the cable and slip them into the pockets. *Anyone can do it.*

And, as everyone knows, "Jiffy" Curtains have the supreme advantage of compactness. They fold without rolling or bending the celluloid lights, which is one reason why they last longer and always look better. You know celluloid should never be rolled.

Note the neat lights of celluloid, with the narrow strips of fabric between, giving you the widest possible range of vision.

Car manufacturers know, just as everybody else knows, that "Jiffy" Curtains are the best, and always the most sightly.

The "Jiffy" license tag, sewed on the left rear curtain, identifies the genuine "Jiffy" Curtains.

JIFFY AUTO CURTAIN COMPANY
DETROIT, MICH.